FAST FEEDBACK

Second Edition

By Bruce Tulgan

HRD PRESS
Amherst, Massachusetts

≡ CONTENTS ≡

This book is dedicated to my loving parents, Henry and Norma Tulgan, with all my love.

≡ ACKNOWLEDGMENTS ≡

FIRST AND FOREMOST, many thanks to the thousands of incredible people who have shared with us over the years the lessons of their experiences with managers in the workplace. Each interview has been a profound learning experience, and I am grateful to every single one of you who took the time to share your voice. Without your insights, there would be no Rainmaker-Thinking.

Many thanks also to Susan Haney, an old friend and associate here at RainmakerThinking, who worked hard on putting the FAST Feedback concepts in the form of a four-hour training program complete with participant workbook, practical tools, leader's guide, vignette-driven videos, Power Point presentation, and more. Working closely with Susan on the FAST Feedback program led me to write this second, revised edition of *FAST Feedback*. For all of your hard work and patience, Susan, thank you.

I am ever grateful to my publisher, Bob Carkhuff, and his staff at HRD Press for our close working relationship and their ongoing confidence in me and in our work at RainmakerThinking. Thank you, Bob, I am honored by your confidence; it is a pleasure working with you and your staff. Special thanks to Mary George for her awesome editing and design work.

To all the business leaders who have brought me in to consult with your organizations, thank you for your faith and for all that you have taught me. And to the tens of thousands who have attended my seminars, thanks for listening, for laughing, for sharing the wisdom of your experience, and for pushing me with the really tough questions; I am grateful for the kindness you have shown and the lessons you have imparted.

To the rest of my colleagues at RainmakerThinking, especially Jeff Coombs, Ruth Gutman, and Mark Kurber, thank you for your hard work and commitment and for your valuable contributions to this enterprise every single day. (Jeff, please, don't ever leave me; if you do, I'll hunt you down.)

To my family and friends, thank you for raising me, for loving me, and for taking care of me. And to my wife, Debby Applegate (nay, Dr. Debby Applegate): the only thing that surpasses my pride in you and your accomplishments is my deep and abiding love for you.

≡ INTRODUCTION ≡

WHAT IS THE DIFFERENCE between a low-performing team and a high-performing team? Nine times out of ten, the difference is a coaching-style manager who knows how to keep individual performers focused and motivated day after day. FAST Feedback is a system that encapsulates the best practices of such managers, based on the continuing workplace-interview research conducted by RainmakerThinking.

The FAST Approach

Fundamental to FAST Feedback is the emphasis on feedback itself, which is, by definition, a *responsive* form of communication. Coaching is an ongoing series of *responses* to someone's performance. *Giving feedback* is the core competency of every coach. According to our research, the FASTer the feedback, the better the coach. Our formula's acronym, FAST, stands

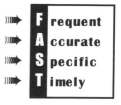

for *frequent, accurate, specific,* and *timely*—the four qualities that employees most often ascribe to feedback from "the best manager [they] ever had" and feedback they need but don't get from most managers.

With this formula as its guide, FAST Feedback takes a direct approach to teaching the key skills and best practices of coaching-style managers. Anyone in a position of supervisory responsibility can learn these essentials and, by applying them in the workplace, contribute to such active improvements as:

▲ Providing employees with regular guidance as needed

▲ Giving employees a greater feeling of being "in the loop"

▲ Building managers' credibility with employees

▲ Increasing the quality of manager–employee interactions

▲ Making responsive coaching the centerpiece of supervisory relationships

▲ Encouraging ongoing results-oriented dialogues between managers and employees

▲ Enabling responsible delegation through regular, built-in review and revision

▲ Linking performance evaluation directly to concrete action steps

▲ Separating performance evaluation from annual raises and promotions

▲ Accelerating turnaround time and increasing productivity

Why a Second Edition So Fast?

Over the last several years I have shared the FAST
Feedback approach in hundreds of speeches for tens of
thousands of business leaders all over the world and in
my work with many of our Fortune 500 clients. In
response to our clients' requests for more resources
to teach managers FAST Feedback skills and best practices, my associate Susan Haney and I recently developed a full-scale management training program, which
will soon join our expanding line of HRD Press products.
I learned a great deal from working on the program. In
fact, it taught me so much that I decided the first edition of *FAST Feedback,* though relatively new, deserved
a revision. My knowledge has grown—and as a result, I
bring you this second edition.

A Brief Look at the Second Edition

You will find all the following features, and more, in the
pages of this guidebook.

- ▲ Clear and simple explanations of the FAST
  approach

- ▲ Examples from real-life workplace case studies

- ▲ Entire chapters devoted to each of the four FAST
  Feedback best practices

- ▲ An informative discussion of the need to turn
  managers into coaches

- ▲ Concrete action steps
- ▲ Room for productive brainstorming
- ▲ Appendices with suggestions and practical tools to help you implement the FAST approach

As you read this second edition, please remember that FAST Feedback is really about the day-to-day relationships between managers and the people they work with most closely—their direct reports and other valued co-workers. This pocket guide, like the FAST Feedback training program, focuses primarily on the four best practices and corresponding skills of the most effective coaching-style managers. If you add these best practices and skills to your management repertoire, you will have the essential tools for transforming your relationships with those you manage and consistently bringing out the very best performance they have to offer.

☛ STOP

Take a Moment to Reflect . . .

BEFORE YOU BEGIN CHAPTER 1, please take a moment
to focus on the people with whom you work most
closely. Consider using the space below and on the next
page to list your direct reports (that is, anyone for
whom you have direct supervisory responsibility). If you
have no direct reports, then list co-workers with whom
you work closely and whose contributions you value.

Remember that FAST Feedback is about your working
relationships with these individuals—keep them in mind
as you read the rest of this book.

DIRECT REPORTS/CO-WORKERS

➡

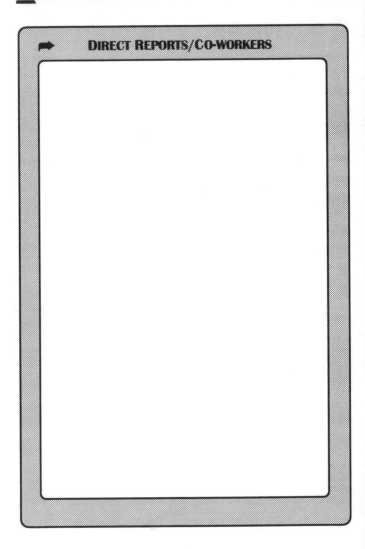

DIRECT REPORTS/CO-WORKERS

Chapter 1

WHAT IS FAST FEEDBACK?

FAST FEEDBACK is a straightforward approach designed to teach anyone in a position of supervisory responsibility the key skills and best practices of the most effective coaching-style managers. This chapter looks at the FAST formula for those skills and practices and its importance in today's workplace. But first, let's address a question that is fundamental here: What exactly *is* feedback?

What Is Feedback?

Feedback is a *reactive* form of communication; that is, a response to some kind of action or input. For example:

▲ An answer to a question

▲ Fulfillment of a request for information

▲ Reply or rebuttal to a point of discussion

▲ Suggestion for work revision

▲ Evaluation of job performance

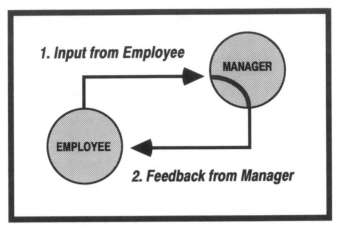

Figure 1. Basic Feedback: A Response to Input

Imagine a game of Ping-Pong: the serve is not feedback, but the return most certainly is, and each subsequent return as well. (The volley ends when a player is unable to provide adequate feedback.) We can apply this analogy to Figure 1: the employee "serves" input to the manager, and the manager "returns" feedback.

Feedback is how we gauge the world's response to our words and actions. When operating in a new environment, people rely on feedback to learn what works and what doesn't—*"How do they do things around here?"*— and so most will actively seek out feedback. The same is true when it comes to dealing with a person or a team for the first time.

Why Is Feedback From Managers Important?

In today's workplace, managerial feedback is a crucial factor in the successful performance of most employees. It answers many of employees' most important questions and helps them do the following:

▲ **Stay focused and motivated**

"Does anybody know I'm here adding value? Does anybody care?"

▲ **Keep moving in the right direction**

"What should I do next?"

▲ **Steadily improve performance**

"What am I doing right? What do I need to improve?"

▲ **Extend the range of individual responsibility without compromising work quality**

"Should I take on more responsibility, or will the quality of my job performance suffer?"

▲ **Find out, in this era of constant flux, what's changing and what's staying the same**

"Is the strategy that worked for me yesterday going to work for me tomorrow?"

What Is FAST Feedback?

FAST Feedback is a practical method for giving employees the kind of feedback they need the most. It is based on the formula FAST, an acronym that stands for:

>)⟩➤ **FREQUENT**
>)⟩➤ **ACCURATE**
>)⟩➤ **SPECIFIC**
>)⟩➤ **TIMELY**

According to our research, these are the four elements employees most often ascribe to feedback from "the best manager [they] ever had." These are also the four elements employees most often say they need *but don't get* in the feedback from most managers. As we keep these important facts in mind, let's take a closer look at each of the FAST elements.

OUR
RESEARCH
REVEALS...

)⟩➤ **FREQUENT**

Some employees need feedback more often than others—each one has a unique "feedback frequency." Giving employees feedback at their individual rates of need is the first key behavior of the best coaching-style managers. *Identifying and tuning in*

to each employee's frequency is the corresponding skill of this behavior.

Every instance of feedback has an effect on the employee's trust and performance. Giving feedback that is correct, balanced, and appropriate is the second key behavior of effective coaching-style managers. Its corresponding skill includes *taking the time to reflect, question assump-*

tions, check facts, and re- hearse the feedback's delivery.

Telling people exactly what they do right and wrong is not specific enough—you must also tell people exactly what next steps are necessary to achieve the best results. This is the third key behavior, with *setting concrete goals and*

deadlines, and providing clear guidelines, as the corresponding skill.

The closer in time feedback follows the performance in question, the more impact the feedback will have on the employee, and the better the chances that any needed improvements will be made. Giving feedback immediately is thus the fourth key behavior of good coaching-style managers. *Effective time management* is its corresponding skill.

Why FAST Feedback Now More Than Ever?

The rapid change and immediacy that largely define our world today are nowhere more evident than in the new JUSTinTIME workplace. Reengineering and restructuring are constant realities as business leaders attempt continually to adapt to chaotic markets, fierce global competition, and unpredictable staffing and resource needs. Everyone is perpetually inexperienced because everything is always new—new people, new information, new products and services, new rules (no rules). In such a workplace, it's hard to know what to expect.

— *What works and what doesn't work TODAY?*

— *How do they do things around here TODAY?*

— *What is changing and what is staying the same TODAY?*

These conditions have made feedback an imperative while, at the same time, leaving traditional feedback in the dust. But FAST Feedback is right there, in sync with the JUSTinTIME workplace.

The FAST approach can keep pace with the JUSTinTIME workplace because it's based on an understanding of what people need *right now* in terms of feedback: quick, quality turnaround on their input, whether that means getting a question answered, performance evaluated, or any other type of feedback delivered.

The truth is, the JUSTinTIME workplace has yielded a JUSTinTIME workforce in need of JUSTinTIME coaching from managers and co-workers. And FAST Feedback can address that need. It offers managers a new and effective way to guide their workers through the difficult terrain of constant change in the new workplace and the new millennium.

Chapter 2

NOT SO FAST . . .

MOST MANAGERS WOULD AGREE that the FAST elements (Frequent, Accurate, Specific, and Timely) should set the standard for feedback given to employees. Indeed, when presented with the FAST approach, many managers insist they *already* give workers such feedback. Surely, some of them really do provide FAST Feedback; however, our interviews with people on the front lines of the workplace tell a much different story, indicating that workplace feedback is *not so FAST,* often missing some or all of the crucial elements of this effective approach.

Employee Complaints and Case Studies

The results of our interviews point to seven major complaints about typical workplace feedback. We'll take a close look at these complaints through seven case studies based on real-life employee examples. A FAST Feedback analysis of each case will also be included.

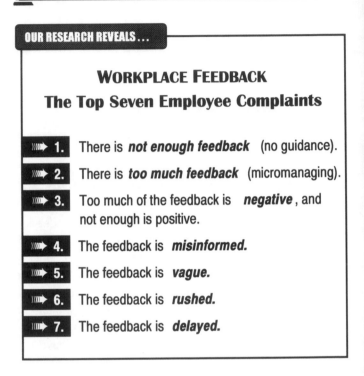

OUR RESEARCH REVEALS...

WORKPLACE FEEDBACK
The Top Seven Employee Complaints

1. There is *not enough feedback* (no guidance).

2. There is *too much feedback* (micromanaging).

3. Too much of the feedback is *negative* , and not enough is positive.

4. The feedback is *misinformed.*

5. The feedback is *vague.*

6. The feedback is *rushed.*

7. The feedback is *delayed.*

1. Not Enough Feedback

CASE STUDY — *Paralegal in a mid-size law firm:*

"I'll try to get one of the lawyers to look at something I'm doing, maybe give me a little guidance, and all I get is 'I don't have time to look at that.' If I leave something I'm working on with one of those guys, they are about as likely to lose it as look at it. If I wait for one of them to get back to me, forget it. . . .

"A lot of times I'll be working on something for the first time, and I have no idea if I'm doing it right until we hear from the lawyers on the other side. They call up one of the lawyers here and chew them out and so I get chewed out, and all I can think of is, If you would have just taken a minute to look at it, we could have avoided all of this hassle."

ANALYSIS. This is an example of a feedback relationship that is totally out of tune with the employee's frequency needs. She asks for guidance repeatedly, but none of her supervisors respond. As a result, she feels unprepared to carry out some of her basic functions and believes her employers do not value her contributions; moreover, her work does not receive the review and revision necessary. Ultimately, the costs go directly to the bottom line because work quality is diminished and the client is unsatisfied. Only then does she receive feedback—when she no longer needs it!

⯈ 2. Too Much Feedback

CASE STUDY — *Staffer in a trade association:*

"My manager would . . . ask me to do . . . a letter for instance. I would do it and he would have corrections or additions. But that process would keep happening several times. He would keep changing his mind, want more words changed. We would spend an hour getting out a routine letter—less than three quarters of a page. . . . It became counterproductive to even have me involved because we would just go back and forth on everything."

ANALYSIS. This is another example of feedback that is out of tune with an employee's frequency needs; however, here the manager is overly involved with the mundane details of the employee's work. He is using feedback as a guise for micromanagement, which never should be done. The result, from the employee's view, is too much feedback.

In viewing this case, we might say that the manager should be more specific and explain from the start precisely what the letter should say—that he needs to delegate a concrete goal with clear parameters. Yet this manager seems unclear about those parameters himself. He keeps changing his mind, requesting additions and revisions, using the employee like a puppet to play out a creative process that he should work through on his own. He is, above all, *entirely* too tangled up in the employee's tasks and responsibilities: her work and his work are not clearly delineated. The manager is therefore out of tune with the employee's frequency needs, virtually distorting feedback into nothing more than a burden.

⟫▶ 3. Too Much Negative Feedback

CASE STUDY — *Information systems consultant:*

"He gives plenty of negative feedback, but never a kind word. . . .

"He will leave me a message on my voice-mail criticizing something if he doesn't like it; but I don't get a message when I do a good job. It's a distraction. I get sidetracked because I am mad."

ANALYSIS. This is an example of a feedback relationship that is so unbalanced it results in inaccurate information; it also probably gives the employee a misleading picture of the manager's actual evaluation of his performance. "No word is good word" doesn't cut it anymore. Employees need to know *exactly* what they are doing right so they can repeat their successes, just as they need to know what they are doing wrong so they can avoid repeating mistakes.

The manager in this case may not realize how much damage he is doing to the employee's morale. But the damage is palpable. The employee reports here that his focus is diminished by anger. That means he is going to be less productive and the quality of his work is likely to suffer.

⟫➤ 4. The Feedback Is Misinformed

CASE STUDY — *Department leader in department store:*

"What I find really unfair is when my boss yells at me because of a customer complaint, without even checking out my side of the story. One time this customer [was] yelling at my cashier because she wouldn't let him return a sweater that is not sold at our store. We have an inventory control system, and we can tell if an item came from our system or not. . . . I go over and tell this customer to stop yelling at my cashier. He writes down our names, [gestures obscenely], and stomps off. The next thing I know the store manager is screaming at me how this guy says he's never going to shop at [our store] again. He didn't shop [here] to begin with."

ANALYSIS. This is another example of inaccurate feedback. Because the store manager failed to check her facts—or at least check the department leader's or cashier's side of the story—she has severely diminished her credibility with this department leader and probably with the cashier as well.

While the department leader was in a good position to witness the interaction between the customer and the cashier, and thus to assess the situation properly—the store manager had no firsthand information. What is more, the department leader relied on the store's inventory control system (a reliable fact check) to determine the appropriate response to give the customer; but the store manager did not utilize this source of information. Even if store policy is "the customer is always right," it was certainly inappropriate for the store manager to scream at the department leader for defending the cashier and enforcing another store policy (not accepting returns purchased from another store). The manager should have . . .

> — checked her facts,
>
> — questioned her assumptions, and
>
> — offered a more suitable response.

⟩⟩▶ 5. Vague Feedback

CASE STUDY — *Temp working in a bank:*

"You know, a pat on the back is great and all too rare, but it still doesn't tell me much. I'd like to know exactly what it is I'm doing right, so I can make sure to keep doing it.

"[My boss] is always trying to make me feel like he appreciates my work—unless he's [angry about something I did]. And then, dirty looks are, you know, [his response. I want to say,] OK, I can see you're really [mad] at me, but tell me what I did wrong so I can fix it or at least not do it again."

— 17 —

ANALYSIS. This is an example of feedback that is given often enough; however, it is not specific enough to be of much use to the employee. The manager in this case is trying to give feedback, but doesn't know exactly how to communicate the details of a performance evaluation or how to delegate concrete "next steps."

At first glance, it seems inaccuracy is the problem here (and the feedback *is* too imprecise to be entirely accurate). But on close inspection, we notice that the manager gives both positive and negative feedback (balanced), and that the employee is not accusing the manager of being wrong or unfair. What she is complaining about is *the lack of specifics* in his feedback: she wants details so she can act on his response.

This manager should be telling the employee . . .

- — exactly what she does wrong (instead of giving her dirty looks),
- — exactly what she does right (instead of giving her pats on the back), and
- — exactly what she should do next (instead of expecting her to figure it out).

He needs to delegate concrete goals and deadlines with clear guidelines and parameters so that his employee, who is so willing to act on feedback, can improve her performance for the benefit of them both.

▸ 6. Rushed Feedback

CASE STUDY — *Merchandise analyst for a retail chain:*

"Everybody is always running around here like crazy because we are super busy; but some people make it much worse because they never slow down long enough to utter a coherent thought. [For instance, my manager will say,] 'You gotta change those sales projections.' And I'll say, 'The projections I gave you yesterday?' And she'll say, 'Not yesterday—I haven't even looked at that.' She's, like, zooming by as we have this exchange, and I'm left there thinking, Gee, maybe you could tell me which projection you're talking about. . . .

"I can track down her assistant or something, and try to figure out what she was talking about, but that doesn't speed things up for anybody. She's in such a hurry, she slows everything down."

ANALYSIS. While this manager is out of sync with her employee's frequency needs, not very accurate, and also somewhat vague, the case is presented primarily as an example of feedback that is untimely because of the manager's lack of time-management skills.

It is ironic but all too common for managers to feel they haven't the time to take action that will ultimately save *lots* of time. Here, time is precious for manager and employee alike, yet the manager's failure to focus for just a few moments on feedback results in a waste of time for them both; she didn't maximize the time she did spend on the interaction, and her employee has to figure out what she was talking about. What is more, by giving feedback only in passing, the manager implies that the feedback is low priority.

This manager needs to plan (daily, weekly, or monthly) specific blocks of time in her schedule, however brief they may be, so she can focus her attention when she provides feedback.

7. Delayed Feedback

CASE STUDY — Graphic designer:

"My boss insists on seeing everything before it goes out of here, and he always has changes. But he takes forever to get back to you, which means our clients are always complaining about the delays. I [can] finish something in half a day and then it will sit on my boss's desk for a week. . . .

"One time he stumbled onto a design that I had given him so long before (months) that nobody could remember which client it was even for. I had to dig through a bunch of old files [to find out]. When I finally got in touch with the client, she had already gone to someone else and the job was over and done with."

ANALYSIS. This is an extreme example of untimely feedback resulting from a manager's lack of time-management and organizational skills. When managers have slow turnaround on reviewing an employee's work in progress, often the only real consequence is a frustrated employee who feels that his or her work is not appreciated. That is consequence enough. In this case, the slow turnaround ends up costing the organization a potentially valuable client as well.

When a manager's review and revision are necessary parts of an employee's regular work process (as is often the case), then timeliness is all the more critical. This manager should give himself a 48-hour rule on reviewing employees' work in progress.

Why Are These Complaints So Common?

Most of the time the problem is a lack of *consistent, focused attention and effort*—the very same things that give effective coaching-style management its power to bring out the best in employees. Many managers are so busy with other work that they neglect integral supervisory responsibilities such as:

▲ Providing upfront guidance

▲ Delegating effectively

▲ Thoroughly revising work in progress

- ▲ Providing detailed appraisal of final results
- ▲ Giving balanced feedback
- ▲ Rewarding high performers

In effect, such managers wish their employees would just manage themselves.

This neglect frequently results in mistakes and problems, even crises, that require the manager's attention *after all*. And when a manager is finally pulled away from scheduled tasks and responsibilities to intervene in the situation, he or she usually expresses displeasure with subordinates. Such expression commonly takes the form of general reproach or instructions for damage control. Then the manager goes back to business as usual, hoping the employees will just supervise themselves until the next mistake, problem, or crisis—when the manager will be needed again . . . after all.

Too often the problem is one of skill. People are not necessarily promoted to positions of supervisory responsibility because they are good at managing people; quite often, it is because they have proven task-related expertise or simply have acquired experience in a department. The result? Plenty of supervising managers out there just don't know how to bring out the best in the people they supervise.

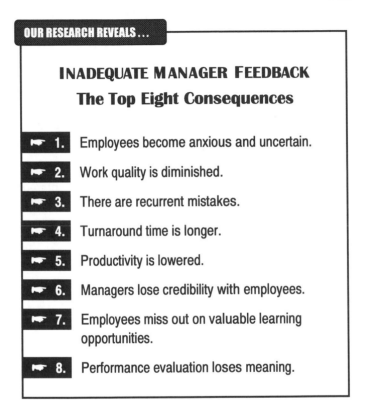

INADEQUATE MANAGER FEEDBACK
The Top Eight Consequences

1. Employees become anxious and uncertain.

2. Work quality is diminished.

3. There are recurrent mistakes.

4. Turnaround time is longer.

5. Productivity is lowered.

6. Managers lose credibility with employees.

7. Employees miss out on valuable learning opportunities.

8. Performance evaluation loses meaning.

INADEQUATE MANAGER FEEDBACK: THE CONSEQUENCES

The results of inadequate feedback are severe, as our list of the top eight consequences illustrates. Without effective feedback—*FAST* Feedback—a workplace is missing a fundamental management tool necessary for any organization's success.

What About Formal Reviews?

Formal reviews vary a great deal in format and style, but any way you slice it, they are creatures from the workplace of the past. Most people go into their six- and twelve-month reviews with two things in mind: *How much is my raise going to be?* and *Am I going to get a promotion?*

Meanwhile, our research shows there are four common complaints about formal reviews:

1. Reviews are almost always conducted too long after the focal performance to be relevant and helpful. This time lag makes it difficult to take action on the matters reviewed, and so those matters are poor reference points for learning.

2. Managers and employees tend to use the review process to protect their own interests; therefore, reviews are usually not as candid as they should be.

3. Reviews often reflect personality issues and internal politics, not performance evaluations.

4. Sometimes managers do not take reviews seriously enough to yield thorough performance evaluations—they prepare the reviews at the last minute, do them only because required, or treat them as pro forma events.

I am not suggesting that organizations should do away with formal six- and twelve-month reviews. Indeed, when reviews are done well and taken seriously, they provide employees and managers with important long-term performance benchmarks. However, no matter how well they are carried out and how seriously they are taken, formal reviews will never be a replacement for the kind of day-to-day coaching-style feedback that most employees need in the new JUSTinTIME workplace in order to perform at their highest level.

Chapter 3

REALITY CHECK
How FAST Is Your Feedback?

ONCE AGAIN, let me point out that if you asked a roomful of managers about feedback (as I have done on many occasions), most would agree that the FAST elements should set the standard for workplace feedback; further, most would claim they already give employees such feedback. What do *you* think about the necessity for frequent, accurate, specific, and timely feedback? Do you already provide your direct reports and valued co-workers with FAST feedback?

This chapter offers a self-evaluation that will help you assess whether your feedback does indeed measure up to the FAST standard. Also included is a second evaluation for assessing feedback *you have received* from a manager. Together, these two exercises will bring you even closer to understanding what frequent, accurate, specific, and timely feedback means *in practice.* And the practice of FAST Feedback is the ultimate goal of this approach.

1. The FAST Self-Evaluation

This self-evaluation is designed to help you identify your strengths and weaknesses as a feedback provider and improve your areas of weakness. It requires that you take the following steps:

1. Recall an instance when you gave feedback to a direct report or other valued co-worker.

2. Objectively assess that feedback by answering 12 evaluation questions.

3. Score the assessment to see how FAST your feedback was.

4. Brainstorm actions for improving the quality of your feedback.

Consider using the work space in the evaluation's first section to record details of the feedback episode you have selected for your focus. This may help you with your recollections during work on Step 2, the feedback assessment.

☛ **Please note that an additional copy of the self-evaluation can be found in Appendix B.**

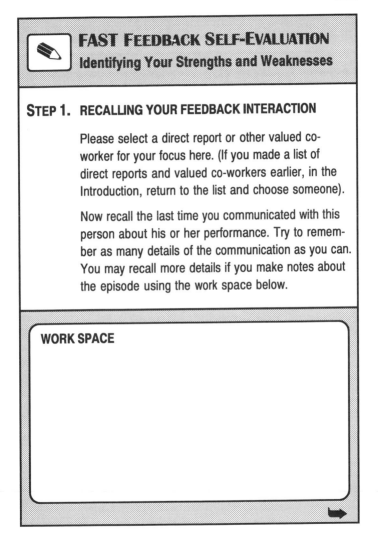

FAST FEEDBACK SELF-EVALUATION
Identifying Your Strengths and Weaknesses

STEP 1. **RECALLING YOUR FEEDBACK INTERACTION**

Please select a direct report or other valued co-worker for your focus here. (If you made a list of direct reports and valued co-workers earlier, in the Introduction, return to the list and choose someone).

Now recall the last time you communicated with this person about his or her performance. Try to remember as many details of the communication as you can. You may recall more details if you make notes about the episode using the work space below.

WORK SPACE

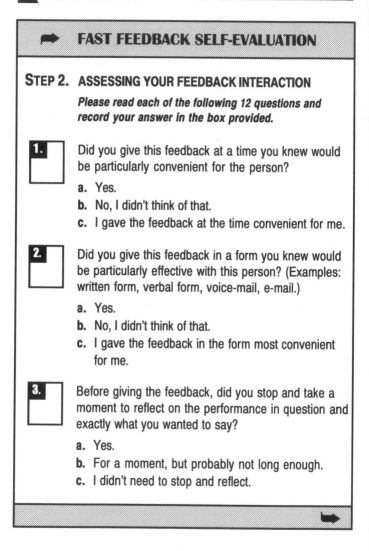

➡ **FAST FEEDBACK SELF-EVALUATION**

STEP 2. ASSESSING YOUR FEEDBACK INTERACTION

*Please read each of the following 12 questions and
record your answer in the box provided.*

1. Did you give this feedback at a time you knew would
be particularly convenient for the person?

   a. Yes.
   b. No, I didn't think of that.
   c. I gave the feedback at the time convenient for me.

2. Did you give this feedback in a form you knew would
be particularly effective with this person? (Examples:
written form, verbal form, voice-mail, e-mail.)

   a. Yes.
   b. No, I didn't think of that.
   c. I gave the feedback in the form most convenient
      for me.

3. Before giving the feedback, did you stop and take a
moment to reflect on the performance in question and
exactly what you wanted to say?

   a. Yes.
   b. For a moment, but probably not long enough.
   c. I didn't need to stop and reflect.

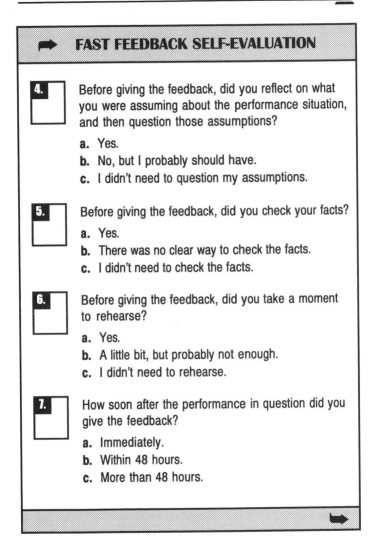

➡ **FAST FEEDBACK SELF-EVALUATION**

4. Before giving the feedback, did you reflect on what you were assuming about the performance situation, and then question those assumptions?

a. Yes.

b. No, but I probably should have.

c. I didn't need to question my assumptions.

5. Before giving the feedback, did you check your facts?

a. Yes.

b. There was no clear way to check the facts.

c. I didn't need to check the facts.

6. Before giving the feedback, did you take a moment to rehearse?

a. Yes.

b. A little bit, but probably not enough.

c. I didn't need to rehearse.

7. How soon after the performance in question did you give the feedback?

a. Immediately.

b. Within 48 hours.

c. More than 48 hours.

➡

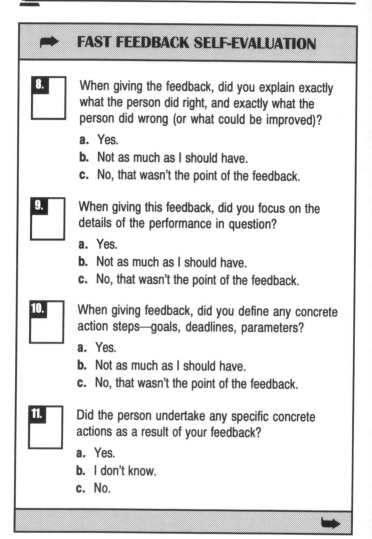

8.

When giving the feedback, did you explain exactly what the person did right, and exactly what the person did wrong (or what could be improved)?

a. Yes.
b. Not as much as I should have.
c. No, that wasn't the point of the feedback.

9.

When giving this feedback, did you focus on the details of the performance in question?

a. Yes.
b. Not as much as I should have.
c. No, that wasn't the point of the feedback.

10.

When giving feedback, did you define any concrete action steps—goals, deadlines, parameters?

a. Yes.
b. Not as much as I should have.
c. No, that wasn't the point of the feedback.

11.

Did the person undertake any specific concrete actions as a result of your feedback?

a. Yes.
b. I don't know.
c. No.

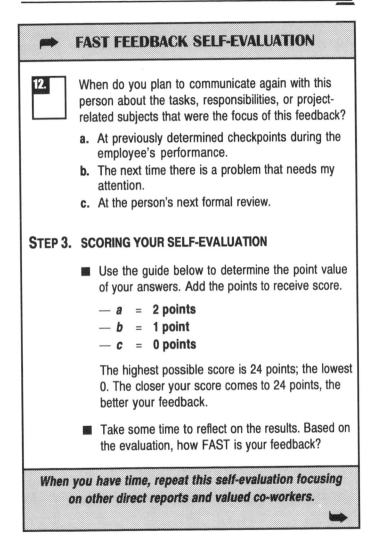

➡ **FAST FEEDBACK SELF-EVALUATION**

12. When do you plan to communicate again with this person about the tasks, responsibilities, or project-related subjects that were the focus of this feedback?

a. At previously determined checkpoints during the employee's performance.

b. The next time there is a problem that needs my attention.

c. At the person's next formal review.

STEP 3. **SCORING YOUR SELF-EVALUATION**

■ Use the guide below to determine the point value of your answers. Add the points to receive score.

— *a* = **2 points**
— *b* = **1 point**
— *c* = **0 points**

The highest possible score is 24 points; the lowest 0. The closer your score comes to 24 points, the better your feedback.

■ Take some time to reflect on the results. Based on the evaluation, how FAST is your feedback?

When you have time, repeat this self-evaluation focusing on other direct reports and valued co-workers.

➡

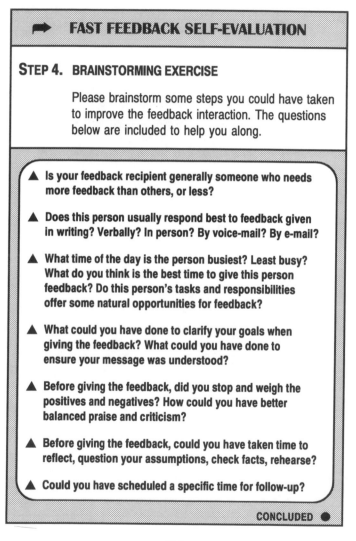

➡ **FAST FEEDBACK SELF-EVALUATION**

STEP 4. BRAINSTORMING EXERCISE

Please brainstorm some steps you could have taken to improve the feedback interaction. The questions below are included to help you along.

▲ Is your feedback recipient generally someone who needs more feedback than others, or less?

▲ Does this person usually respond best to feedback given in writing? Verbally? In person? By voice-mail? By e-mail?

▲ What time of the day is the person busiest? Least busy? What do you think is the best time to give this person feedback? Do this person's tasks and responsibilities offer some natural opportunities for feedback?

▲ What could you have done to clarify your goals when giving the feedback? What could you have done to ensure your message was understood?

▲ Before giving the feedback, did you stop and weigh the positives and negatives? How could you have better balanced praise and criticism?

▲ Before giving the feedback, could you have taken time to reflect, question your assumptions, check facts, rehearse?

▲ Could you have scheduled a specific time for follow-up?

CONCLUDED ●

2. The FAST Evaluation: Manager Feedback

This evaluation is designed to help you gain some valuable perspective by assessing feedback you have received from a manager. It requires that you take the following steps:

1. Recall an instance when you received feedback from a senior manager you report to now or have reported to in the past.

2. Objectively assess that feedback by answering 12 evaluation questions.

3. Score the assessment to see how FAST your manager's feedback was.

Consider using the work space in the evaluation's first section to record details of the feedback episode you have chosen for your focus. This may help you with your recollections during work on Step 2, the assessment of your manager's feedback.

☞ **Please note that an additional copy of the evaluation can be found in Appendix B.**

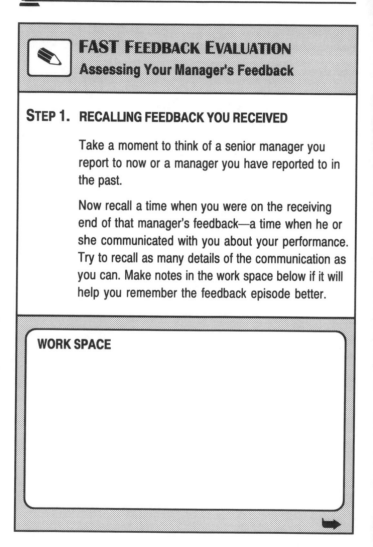

FAST FEEDBACK EVALUATION
Assessing Your Manager's Feedback

STEP 1. RECALLING FEEDBACK YOU RECEIVED

Take a moment to think of a senior manager you report to now or a manager you have reported to in the past.

Now recall a time when you were on the receiving end of that manager's feedback—a time when he or she communicated with you about your performance. Try to recall as many details of the communication as you can. Make notes in the work space below if it will help you remember the feedback episode better.

WORK SPACE

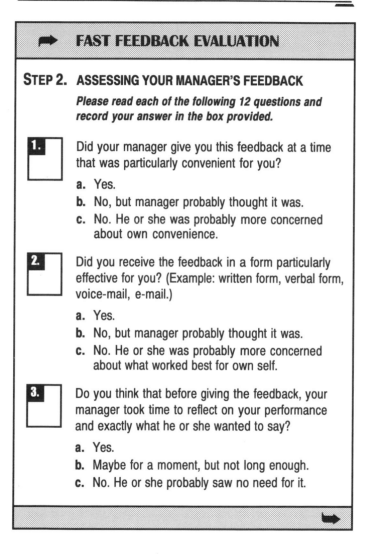

➡ **FAST FEEDBACK EVALUATION**

Step 2. Assessing Your Manager's Feedback

Please read each of the following 12 questions and record your answer in the box provided.

1. Did your manager give you this feedback at a time that was particularly convenient for you?

  a. Yes.
  b. No, but manager probably thought it was.
  c. No. He or she was probably more concerned about own convenience.

2. Did you receive the feedback in a form particularly effective for you? (Example: written form, verbal form, voice-mail, e-mail.)

  a. Yes.
  b. No, but manager probably thought it was.
  c. No. He or she was probably more concerned about what worked best for own self.

3. Do you think that before giving the feedback, your manager took time to reflect on your performance and exactly what he or she wanted to say?

  a. Yes.
  b. Maybe for a moment, but not long enough.
  c. No. He or she probably saw no need for it.

➡

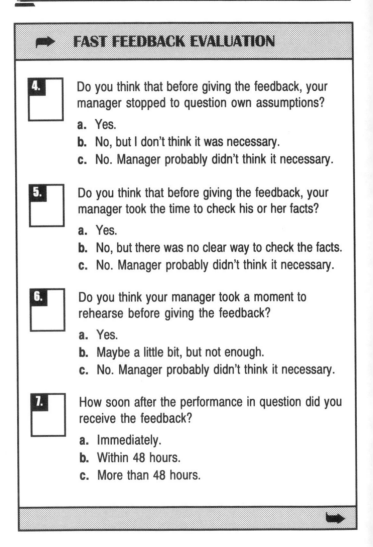

➡ **FAST FEEDBACK EVALUATION**

4. Do you think that before giving the feedback, your manager stopped to question own assumptions?

   a. Yes.
   b. No, but I don't think it was necessary.
   c. No. Manager probably didn't think it necessary.

5. Do you think that before giving the feedback, your manager took the time to check his or her facts?

   a. Yes.
   b. No, but there was no clear way to check the facts.
   c. No. Manager probably didn't think it necessary.

6. Do you think your manager took a moment to rehearse before giving the feedback?

   a. Yes.
   b. Maybe a little bit, but not enough.
   c. No. Manager probably didn't think it necessary.

7. How soon after the performance in question did you receive the feedback?

   a. Immediately.
   b. Within 48 hours.
   c. More than 48 hours.

➡

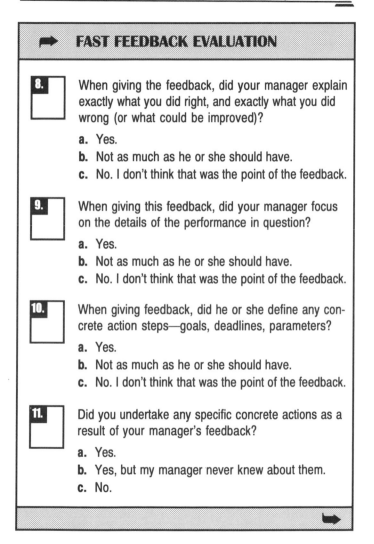

➡ FAST FEEDBACK EVALUATION

8. When giving the feedback, did your manager explain exactly what you did right, and exactly what you did wrong (or what could be improved)?

a. Yes.

b. Not as much as he or she should have.

c. No. I don't think that was the point of the feedback.

9. When giving this feedback, did your manager focus on the details of the performance in question?

a. Yes.

b. Not as much as he or she should have.

c. No. I don't think that was the point of the feedback.

10. When giving feedback, did he or she define any concrete action steps—goals, deadlines, parameters?

a. Yes.

b. Not as much as he or she should have.

c. No. I don't think that was the point of the feedback.

11. Did you undertake any specific concrete actions as a result of your manager's feedback?

a. Yes.

b. Yes, but my manager never knew about them.

c. No.

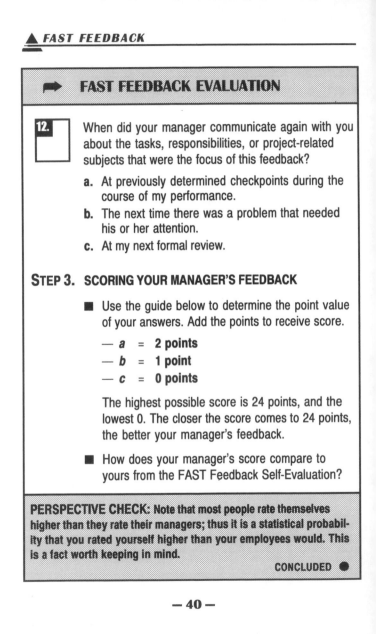

➡ FAST FEEDBACK EVALUATION

12. When did your manager communicate again with you about the tasks, responsibilities, or project-related subjects that were the focus of this feedback?

a. At previously determined checkpoints during the course of my performance.

b. The next time there was a problem that needed his or her attention.

c. At my next formal review.

STEP 3. SCORING YOUR MANAGER'S FEEDBACK

■ Use the guide below to determine the point value of your answers. Add the points to receive score.

— *a* = **2 points**
— *b* = **1 point**
— *c* = **0 points**

The highest possible score is 24 points, and the lowest 0. The closer the score comes to 24 points, the better your manager's feedback.

■ How does your manager's score compare to yours from the FAST Feedback Self-Evaluation?

PERSPECTIVE CHECK: Note that most people rate themselves higher than they rate their managers; thus it is a statistical probability that you rated yourself higher than your employees would. This is a fact worth keeping in mind.

CONCLUDED ●

Chapter 4

FREQUENT FEEDBACK

Tuning In to Each Person's Unique Needs

THE FIRST KEY to the FAST approach is giving feedback that is *frequent.* It is also the first key behavior of the best coaching-style managers, based on our research.

Frequent Feedback: Definition

What does the word *frequent* really mean? Typically, its dictionary definition is "happening often or at short intervals." But how short is a short interval? And in the context of feedback, how often is often enough?

> ⟫ *Remember . . .*
> **Frequent feedback ensures that employees are given feedback at their unique rates of need.**

Our research tells us that the majority of managers do not provide feedback often enough—that is, in most cases the intervals between feedback interactions are too long. However, our research also shows that a substantial percentage of managers err on the other side, providing feedback *too often.* Managers in this position give feedback at intervals so short that they hardly feel like intervals—a problem that can easily lead to micromanagement. Thus, while most managers should be giving more feedback, *frequent* cannot mean "the more often, the better" or "the shorter the intervals between feedback interactions, the better."

THE ANSWER? IT'S ALL RELATIVE

By turning to the related term *frequency* and focusing on its more scientific definitions, we come much closer to understanding what frequent feedback really means. At first glance, these definitions seem to have little to do with feedback. For example:

— *The number of cycles per second of an alternating electric current*

— *The number of complete oscillations per second of an electromagnetic wave*

— *The number of sound waves per second produced by a sounding body*

But together, they draw attention to the *relative* nature of frequency, the fact that it *differs from case to case;* they also convey that frequency is *measurable.*

In terms of FAST Feedback, then, *frequency* means "the number of feedback opportunities generated by an

> ▲ **FAST Definitions**
>
> **Frequency:**
> *The number of feedback opportunities produced by an employee's performance.*
>
> **Frequent Feedback:**
> *Feedback that is in tune with the employee's unique frequency.*

employee's performance." This means that every employee has a unique frequency when it comes to needing feedback. Consequently, managers should give feedback which is "in tune" with the employee's frequency.

Keep in mind: Feedback is, by definition, a process that employees initiate, and they will naturally try to regulate the frequency of their feedback requests depending on their changing needs and the extent to which managers are responding to those needs.

When employees receive feedback that is in tune with their needs (given at the proper frequency), they grow more capable and confident. As they do, they are likely to earn responsibility for tasks and projects requiring longer work periods and further deadlines. Such development usually coincides with a gradual *decrease* in the amount of feedback necessary (a change in frequency).

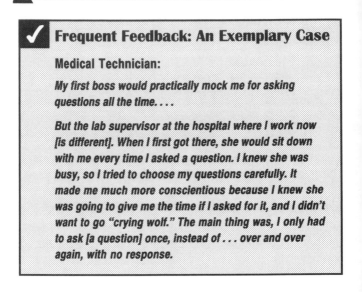

✓ Frequent Feedback: An Exemplary Case

Medical Technician:

My first boss would practically mock me for asking questions all the time. . . .

But the lab supervisor at the hospital where I work now [is different]. When I first got there, she would sit down with me every time I asked a question. I knew she was busy, so I tried to choose my questions carefully. It made me much more conscientious because I knew she was going to give me the time if I asked for it, and I didn't want to go "crying wolf." The main thing was, I only had to ask [a question] once, instead of . . . over and over again, with no response.

OUT-OF-TUNE FEEDBACK: THE TOP FIVE CAUSES

Our research has revealed five major causes of out-of-tune feedback. The first cause on our list, "The manager bases the timing and manner of the feedback on his or her *own* frequency," is the number one cause in practice *and* the root cause of out-of-tune feedback in general. It underlies other problems such as managers feeling too busy to give feedback or relying too much on formal evaluations. If you address this first cause, you will cut the source of the other listed causes and be well on your way to *in-tune* feedback. The guidelines that follow our list will give you further assistance.

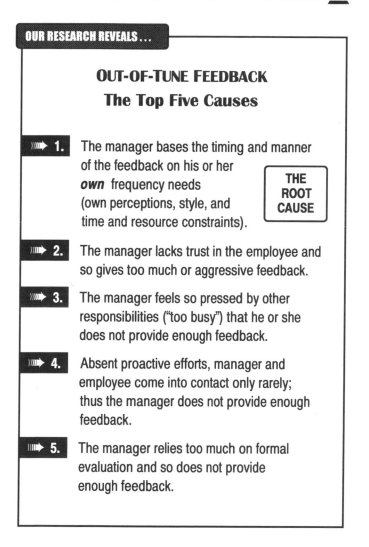

OUR RESEARCH REVEALS...

OUT-OF-TUNE FEEDBACK
The Top Five Causes

1. The manager bases the timing and manner of the feedback on his or her *own* frequency needs (own perceptions, style, and time and resource constraints).

> THE
> ROOT
> CAUSE

2. The manager lacks trust in the employee and so gives too much or aggressive feedback.

3. The manager feels so pressed by other responsibilities ("too busy") that he or she does not provide enough feedback.

4. Absent proactive efforts, manager and employee come into contact only rarely; thus the manager does not provide enough feedback.

5. The manager relies too much on formal evaluation and so does not provide enough feedback.

GUIDELINES

Getting In Tune With Employee Frequency

1. **Recognize every employee's unique frequency.**

Different employees need different amounts and different types of feedback, and these factors are likely to vary over time. Think about each person who reports to you, and evaluate how much feedback he or she needs.

2. **Note that tasks and responsibilities yield feedback opportunities.**

There are *abundant* opportunities to give feedback. Every task, responsibility, and relevant employee input (questions, requests, intermediate or final results, instances of performance observed firsthand or reported) afford you a chance to give the employee a constructive response.

Keep in mind that feedback can be . . .

— *scheduled or unscheduled*

— *given one-on-one or in the presence of others* (e.g., during a team meeting)

— *offered in person or in other ways* (by voice-mail, e-mail, telephone; in writing)

➡ GUIDELINES

Getting In Tune With Employee Frequency

3. **Tune in to feedback opportunities.**

Each employee's frequency is determined by the employee's key tasks, responsibilities, and other relevant inputs. Some tasks, responsibilities, and other inputs require feedback more often than others; at different times than others; in different forms than others. Seize the opportunities that work best in each situation.

4. **When in doubt, give feedback; then pay close attention to the result.**

Don't let doubt stop you—give the feedback you think is needed, see how the employee responds, and then adjust the feedback accordingly. It may take a little time to get in tune with each employee, but eventually you will.

Remember, you can always ask for feedback on your feedback.

CONCLUDED ●

EXERCISE 1: Giving Frequent Feedback

The following two-part exercise will help you provide people with the amount of feedback they really need. Part 1 asks you to list your direct reports or other valued co-workers and then assess each one's general feedback-frequency needs. Part 2 requires that you select a direct report or other valued co-worker for a more intensive assessment of needs.

The exercise focuses your attention on two highly important areas of the *Frequent* element, namely:

▲ Understanding the relative nature of frequency

▲ Tuning in to the unique frequency of each individual

The exercise is accompanied by two handy worksheets that make completion easier and reinforce learning. You can return to this exercise, in full or part, whenever you need to tune in to the feedback needs of employees.

☞ **Please note that an additional copy of each exercise can be found in Appendix C.**

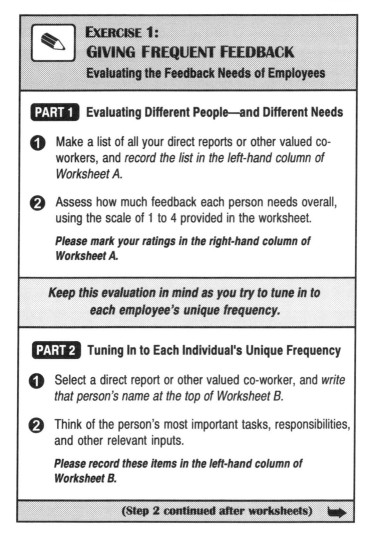

EXERCISE 1:
GIVING FREQUENT FEEDBACK
Evaluating the Feedback Needs of Employees

PART 1 Evaluating Different People—and Different Needs

1 Make a list of all your direct reports or other valued co-workers, and *record the list in the left-hand column of Worksheet A.*

2 Assess how much feedback each person needs overall, using the scale of 1 to 4 provided in the worksheet.

Please mark your ratings in the right-hand column of Worksheet A.

Keep this evaluation in mind as you try to tune in to each employee's unique frequency.

PART 2 Tuning In to Each Individual's Unique Frequency

1 Select a direct report or other valued co-worker, and *write that person's name at the top of Worksheet B.*

2 Think of the person's most important tasks, responsibilities, and other relevant inputs.

Please record these items in the left-hand column of Worksheet B.

(Step 2 continued after worksheets) ➡

Exercise 1 — Worksheet A

Overall, how often do you think each direct report /co-worker needs feedback? Please circle your answer using this scale:

RATING SCALE

1. **Very Often**
2. **Somewhat Often**
3. **Somewhat Rarely**
4. **Very Rarely**

DIRECT REPORTS/VALUED CO-WORKERS	RATING
	1 2 3 4
	1 2 3 4
	1 2 3 4
	1 2 3 4
	1 2 3 4
	1 2 3 4
	1 2 3 4
	1 2 3 4
	1 2 3 4
	1 2 3 4
	1 2 3 4
	1 2 3 4

Exercise 1 — Worksheet B

NAME: _____
(Direct Report/Valued Co-Worker)

How often do you think this person needs feedback on each task, responsibility, input? Please circle your answer using this scale:

RATING SCALE

1. More than once a day
2. Once a day
3. More than once a week
4. Once a week
5. Once every 2 weeks
6. Once a month

TASKS, RESPONSIBILITIES, INPUTS	RATING
1.	1 2 3 4 5 6
2.	1 2 3 4 5 6
3.	1 2 3 4 5 6

Go on to next page

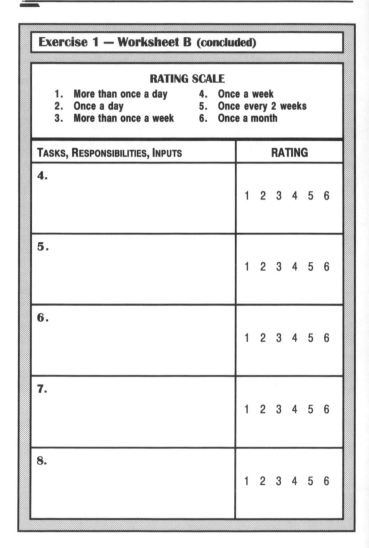

Exercise 1 — Worksheet B (concluded)

RATING SCALE

1. More than once a day
2. Once a day
3. More than once a week
4. Once a week
5. Once every 2 weeks
6. Once a month

TASKS, RESPONSIBILITIES, INPUTS	RATING
4.	1 2 3 4 5 6
5.	1 2 3 4 5 6
6.	1 2 3 4 5 6
7.	1 2 3 4 5 6
8.	1 2 3 4 5 6

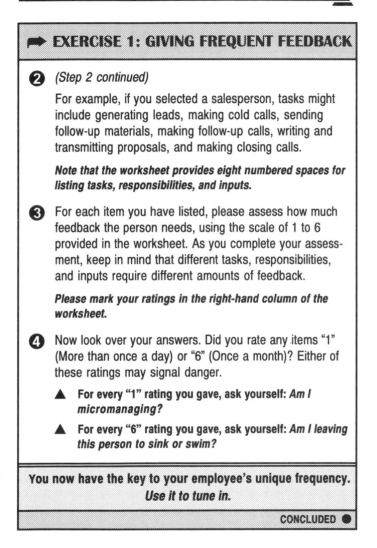

➡ **EXERCISE 1: GIVING FREQUENT FEEDBACK**

❷ *(Step 2 continued)*

For example, if you selected a salesperson, tasks might include generating leads, making cold calls, sending follow-up materials, making follow-up calls, writing and transmitting proposals, and making closing calls.

Note that the worksheet provides eight numbered spaces for listing tasks, responsibilities, and inputs.

❸ For each item you have listed, please assess how much feedback the person needs, using the scale of 1 to 6 provided in the worksheet. As you complete your assessment, keep in mind that different tasks, responsibilities, and inputs require different amounts of feedback.

Please mark your ratings in the right-hand column of the worksheet.

❹ Now look over your answers. Did you rate any items "1" (More than once a day) or "6" (Once a month)? Either of these ratings may signal danger.

▲ For every "1" rating you gave, ask yourself: *Am I micromanaging?*

▲ For every "6" rating you gave, ask yourself: *Am I leaving this person to sink or swim?*

You now have the key to your employee's unique frequency. *Use it to tune in.*

CONCLUDED ●

FAST Tips . . . for Giving Frequent Feedback

Here are some FAST tips that will help ensure your feedback is in tune with the unique frequency of each employee. Use the space that concludes this chapter to add your own suggestions.

1. As a general rule, err on the side of more feedback rather than less.

2. Plan to seize the feedback opportunities that present themselves regularly, day by day.

3. Even more important, be prepared to think fast and seize the ad hoc opportunities for feedback that present themselves only rarely.

4. Be sure to include feedback whenever you review works in progress or final results.

5. Build some feedback into routine meetings.

6. Add some feedback even to routine memoranda.

7. Offer feedback whenever you are an eyewitness to a significant performance.

8. Make feedback a priority, and make time for it.

9. Create a standard process for direct reports to request feedback from you, and reward employees when they do request feedback.

10. Give feedback in a manner and form that is not only convenient for the person on the receiving end, but also convenient for you.

YOUR OWN FAST TIPS:

☰ Chapter 5 ☰

ACCURATE FEEDBACK
Thoughtful, Balanced, and True

THE SECOND KEY to the FAST approach is giving feedback that is accurate. It is also the second key behavior of the most effective coaching-style managers, based on our extensive research.

The Importance of Accurate Feedback

First and foremost: The *Accurate* element is critical because every time a manager provides an employee with feedback, his or her credibility is on the line; giving feedback that an employee perceives as inaccurate (off-base, unfair, unbalanced, or factually wrong) is a sure way to undermine

> ⟫⟫ *Remember . . .*
> **Accurate feedback ensures employees receive feedback that is correct, balanced, and appropriate.**

that credibility, particularly if the manager is evaluating an employee's job performance. On the other hand,

▲ Importance of Accurate Feedback: KEY POINTS

1. *It builds and sustains managers' credibility with employees.*

2. *It is a linchpin of quality control.*

3. *It has a significant impact on incentives, training needs assessment, and leadership development.*

employees come to trust and value managers who regularly provide feedback that is thoughtful, balanced, and true. Managers who take the time to be thorough, sensitive, and instructive earn reputations as the best managers—knowledgeable, skillful, fair, and wise. They are often looked to as mentors.

Second: Accuracy is important because employees will use a manager's performance evaluation to measure what they are doing right (and thus should continue doing) and what they are doing wrong (and thus need to improve). That's why, before examining performance, you need to stop and do the following:

▲ Reflect on what you are about to say

▲ Question your assumptions

▲ Double-check the facts

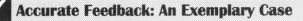

> ✔ **Accurate Feedback: An Exemplary Case**
>
> **Accountant:**
>
> *This one guy was like a coach to me. He'd go over my draft and he could see right away whether I was up to speed. If not, he could see which parts I got and which parts I didn't quite get. Then he'd zero in on the parts that I didn't get and really explain [them]. It was obvious this guy is great at what he does, and you can tell that from the way he teaches.*

▲ Ensure that you are about to move the employee in the *right* direction, not the wrong one

Accurate feedback is a linchpin of quality control.

Finally: The accuracy of managerial feedback has a significant impact on three crucial areas:

1. Rewards and incentives
2. Training needs assessment
3. Leadership development

Rewards and incentives: Remember, one of the reasons why performance evaluation is used at all is so high performers can be identified and rewarded and lower performers given incentives to improve. When feedback is inaccurate, the wrong people are rewarded, and the incentive system is weakened.

Training needs assessment: What is more, employees use feedback to clarify their professional development needs, and thus, inaccurate feedback can lead employees away from the skills and knowledge they need the most and toward training that is inappropriate or unnecessary.

Leadership development: Employees and managers should and do attempt to use managerial feedback to identify high performers worthy of more responsibility and, often, increased authority as well. For this reason, inaccurate feedback can result in a misallocation of leadership-development resources.

INACCURATE FEEDBACK: THE TOP FIVE CAUSES

Our research has revealed there are five major causes of inaccurate feedback. These findings emphasize why it is vital for managers to invest some time in preparing for feedback delivery, and point up the problem which employees encounter when managers rush through that delivery. They also underscore the need to double-check facts (in case your source was unreliable) and to review assumptions (so that you don't leap to conclusions).

OUR RESEARCH REVEALS...

INACCURATE FEEDBACK
The Top Five Causes

1. The manager doesn't take enough time to *prepare* for giving the feedback.

2. The manager *rushes through the delivery* of the feedback.

3. The subject matter of the feedback is emotionally charged.

4. The manager focuses disproportionately on the negative because the manager only gives feedback when there is a problem.

5. The manager bases feedback on information from unreliable sources.

Avoid the pitfalls that result in inaccurate feedback by keeping to the guidelines presented next. They will help you ensure that your feedback is indeed thoughtful, balanced, and true—the kind of feedback that the best coaching-style managers give their employees.

GUIDELINES

Giving Feedback That Is Correct, Balanced, and Appropriate

1.

Remember, your credibility is on the line.

Every time you give a person accurate feedback you have an opportunity to build trust and move that person in the right direction. Inaccurate feedback will surely diminish trust and move that person in the wrong direction.

2.

In preparing to give feedback, stop and reflect on the content of the feedback.

Make sure your feedback is thoughtful by taking a moment to question your assumptions and check your facts.

What do you really know about the matter?

Also examine the sources of information underlying the feedback.

Are these sources reliable?
Should they be double-checked?

➡ GUIDELINES
Giving Feedback That Is Thoughtful, Balanced, and True

3. **Balance praise and criticism.**

When the feedback's point is criticism:
first, think about the person's *valuable* contributions. You might write down instances of more praiseworthy performance and consider mentioning some positives before turning to the negatives. Above all, focus criticism on *the performance,* not the person.

When the feedback's point is praise:
be careful about *over* praising, especially when the person clearly has room for improvement. Although employees like nothing more than praise, it is to their benefit to be given feedback with *a balance* of praise and criticism.

4. **Refine your message and rehearse.**

Take the time to prepare your feedback message. If the feedback will be in written form, construct a first draft. If it will be delivered verbally, repeat it to yourself at least once before delivering it to the employee. (Consider writing yourself a "script.")

CONCLUDED ●

EXERCISE 2: Giving Accurate Feedback

The following exercise is an effective tool for preparing to give others feedback. It requires that you select a direct report or other valued co-worker and review and refine the feedback you intend to deliver.

The exercise focuses your attention on three highly important areas of the *Accurate* FAST Feedback element, namely:

▲ Checking your facts

▲ Balancing positives (praise) and negatives (constructive criticism)

▲ Refining your message

The exercise is accompanied by a handy worksheet that makes completion easier and reinforces learning. Come back to this worksheet whenever you need to provide someone with feedback.

> ☛ **Please note that an additional copy of this exercise can be found in Appendix C.**

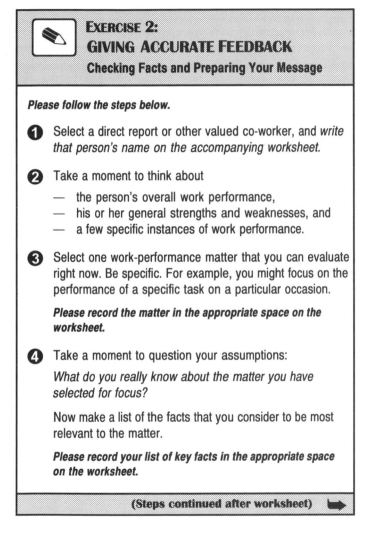

EXERCISE 2:
GIVING ACCURATE FEEDBACK
Checking Facts and Preparing Your Message

Please follow the steps below.

1 Select a direct report or other valued co-worker, and *write that person's name on the accompanying worksheet.*

2 Take a moment to think about

— the person's overall work performance,
— his or her general strengths and weaknesses, and
— a few specific instances of work performance.

3 Select one work-performance matter that you can evaluate right now. Be specific. For example, you might focus on the performance of a specific task on a particular occasion.

Please record the matter in the appropriate space on the worksheet.

4 Take a moment to question your assumptions:

What do you really know about the matter you have selected for focus?

Now make a list of the facts that you consider to be most relevant to the matter.

Please record your list of key facts in the appropriate space on the worksheet.

(Steps continued after worksheet) ➡

✎ Exercise 2 — Worksheet

FEEDBACK RECIPIENT: _____
(Direct Report/Valued Co-Worker)

THE PERFORMANCE MATTER UNDER FOCUS

1. RELEVANT FACTS ABOUT THE MATTER *Please list facts below.*	2. SOURCE OF EACH FACT *List sources; then note how sure you are about each fact.*

Go on to next page

Exercise 2 — Worksheet (concluded)

POSITIVES (PRAISE)	NEGATIVES (CRITICISM)
What elements merit praise?	*What elements require constructive criticism?*

REFINING THE MESSAGE

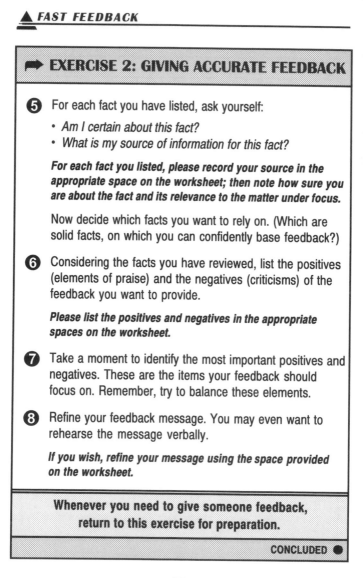

➡ EXERCISE 2: GIVING ACCURATE FEEDBACK

⑤ For each fact you have listed, ask yourself:

- *Am I certain about this fact?*
- *What is my source of information for this fact?*

For each fact you listed, please record your source in the appropriate space on the worksheet; then note how sure you are about the fact and its relevance to the matter under focus.

Now decide which facts you want to rely on. (Which are solid facts, on which you can confidently base feedback?)

⑥ Considering the facts you have reviewed, list the positives (elements of praise) and the negatives (criticisms) of the feedback you want to provide.

Please list the positives and negatives in the appropriate spaces on the worksheet.

⑦ Take a moment to identify the most important positives and negatives. These are the items your feedback should focus on. Remember, try to balance these elements.

⑧ Refine your feedback message. You may even want to rehearse the message verbally.

If you wish, refine your message using the space provided on the worksheet.

Whenever you need to give someone feedback, return to this exercise for preparation.

CONCLUDED ●

FAST Tips . . . for Making Feedback More Accurate

Here are some FAST tips that will help you ensure your feedback is *accurate.* Use the space that concludes this chapter to add your own suggestions.

1. Always stop and take a moment to reflect before providing feedback.

2. Question your assumptions.

3. Check your facts by identifying and evaluating the primary sources of those facts.

4. If you have time, double-check facts against independent sources you know to be reliable.

5. Get a second opinion.

6. In the case of hearsay (the unverified statement of a third party), ask for the employee's own account or get details from a second objective witness.

7. Before giving feedback, take the time to balance positives and negatives, praise and criticism.

8. When delivering the feedback, give more time to the positives than the negatives, and be more emphatic about the positives.

9. Choose your words carefully. If planning to give written feedback, consider working on a first draft. If planning to give verbal feedback, consider writing a script and taking time to rehearse.

10. Stick to the matter under focus: Don't give feedback beyond the specific work product, performance, or query at issue.

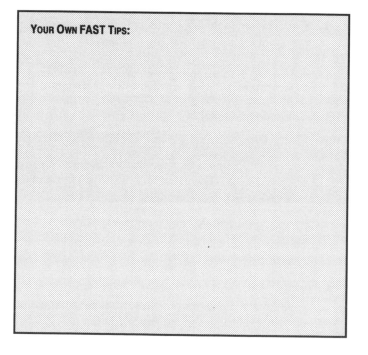

YOUR OWN FAST TIPS:

☰ Chapter 6 ☰

SPECIFIC FEEDBACK
Focusing on Concrete Action Steps

THE THIRD KEY to the FAST approach is giving feedback that is *specific*. This is also the third key behavior of the best coaching-style managers, according to our extensive research.

The Importance of Specific Feedback

The *Specific* element is instrumental to coaching "next steps"—focusing on what needs to happen next. Unlike accurate feedback, which supports evaluation and focuses on what has *already* happened, specific feedback *looks ahead.* Because coaching next steps is the key to coaching anyone in anything,

> ⟫⟫ *Remember . . .*
> Specific feedback helps the recipient define exactly what *next steps* are needed to achieve the best results.

it is the most important aspect of FAST Feedback, and *Specific* the most crucial element.

The Need for Concrete Action Steps

It is vital to understand that evaluation in itself is not coaching. Telling employees exactly what they are doing right and doing wrong simply does not provide enough information to guide them to their best performance. This is why the best coaching-style managers link every instance of performance evaluation to the delegation of concrete goals and deadlines with clear parameters—that is, to *concrete action steps*.

THE PRACTICAL ANGLE ON CONCRETE ACTION STEPS

After receiving your feedback, an employee should know *precisely* what he or she is expected to do next. From a practical perspective, this means three basic things:

1. You must first be clear on the purpose of the feedback:

    What action steps do you want to see happen as a result of the feedback?

2. Your feedback should contain *a recommended next move.* You need to let the employee know what action step to take.

3. Your feedback should contain *enough detail* to enable a next move. This ensures the employee can actually take your recommended step.

> ✓ **Specific Feedback: An Exemplary Case**
>
> **Administrative Assistant:**
>
> *My boss [will] review a letter and say, "This is a good letter. Let's make these five changes right now and then use this as a standard letter in the future." Then the next time [a letter is needed], she might just say to me, "Let's send Mr. Jones and Ms. Smith that standard letter." And I am one step ahead of the game.*

If the employee's input is a question or an information request, all of the basics still apply. If you are unable to supply the needed detail, or are unsure what next move to recommend, then either get advice from a better source or direct the employee's question/information request to a more appropriate source.

If the employee's input is a work in progress under review, you should specify revisions in detail or at least establish clear parameters for revision.

If the employee's input is a final product or past performance, always identify, for future work, the positive elements to repeat and the specific improvements to be made. Whenever possible, set these suggestions in the context of the employee's work in progress (that is, current work), so that you are able to delegate specific goals, deadlines, and parameters—concrete action steps.

Caution: Let me add, beware of turning specific feedback into an excuse for micromanaging. Be careful about nitpicking matters of preference and emphasizing unimportant details. These will distract the employee and water down your message.

ENSURING COMPLETE, EFFECTIVE DELEGATION OF CONCRETE ACTION STEPS

To get the action results you want from the feedback, you need to make certain your delegation is complete and effective. You'll have a better chance for success if you keep to the three simple rules below.

- **First:** Make sure the feedback recipient accepts 100 percent responsibility for the concrete action step when it is assigned.

- **Second:** Make sure the recipient commits explicitly to a time frame or a deadline for the action step.

- **Third:** Make sure the recipient understands from the start all guidelines and parameters that must be observed.

OUR RESEARCH REVEALS ...

FEEDBACK NOT SPECIFIC ENOUGH
The Top Five Causes

))) 1. The manager does not think through his or her reasons for giving the feedback.

))) 2. Too many issues are addressed at once.

))) 3. There is an overemphasis on unimportant details and matters of preference.

))) 4. The manager is focused on *what happened* instead of *what needs to happen next.*

))) 5. The manager fails to ensure the employee has understood the feedback.

FEEDBACK THAT IS NOT SPECIFIC ENOUGH: THE TOP FIVE CAUSES

Our research has revealed five major causes of insufficiently specific feedback. These findings support the caution mentioned earlier and underscore the importance of focusing on concrete action steps. The following guidelines will help you establish and maintain that focus so you can give *sufficiently* specific feedback.

GUIDELINES

Focusing on Concrete Action Steps

1. **Look at evaluation as a chance for action.**

Turn evaluation into action. Remember: every instance of feedback is also an opportunity to delegate—that's what makes it coaching.

2. **Clarify your exact purpose for giving the feedback.**

Before giving the feedback, make sure you know exactly what tangible result you want from giving this particular person this particular feedback at this particular time.

3. **Next, assign concrete action steps.**

This is where you take feedback from evaluation to *action* by delegating specific "next steps." Assign concrete goals and deadlines with clear parameters—concrete action steps.

4. **Finally, get some feedback on your feedback.**

Make sure the feedback recipient understands *exactly* what you expect in the way of next steps. Ask the person to share his or her understanding of the goals, deadlines, and parameters.

EXERCISE 3: Giving Specific Feedback

The following exercise requires that you select a direct report or other valued co-worker and prepare yourself to give that person specific feedback on a performance issue.

The preparation focuses your attention on two highly important areas of the *Specific* FAST Feedback element, namely:

▲ Clarifying the purpose of your feedback

▲ Assigning concrete action steps

The exercise is accompanied by a handy worksheet that makes completion easier and reinforces learning. You can return to the exercise whenever you need to give feedback to make sure your focus is where it should be, on concrete action steps.

> ☞ **Please note that an additional copy of the exercise can be found in Appendix C.**

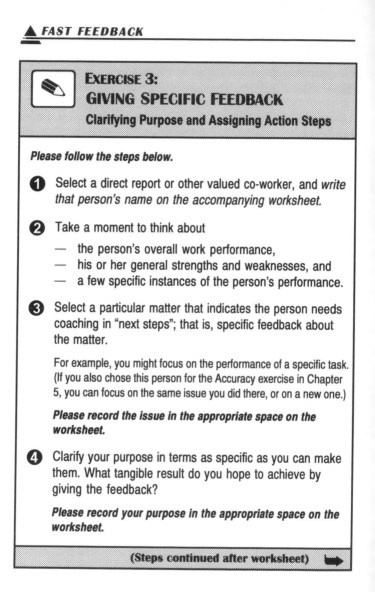

EXERCISE 3:
GIVING SPECIFIC FEEDBACK
Clarifying Purpose and Assigning Action Steps

Please follow the steps below.

1 Select a direct report or other valued co-worker, and *write that person's name on the accompanying worksheet.*

2 Take a moment to think about

— the person's overall work performance,
— his or her general strengths and weaknesses, and
— a few specific instances of the person's performance.

3 Select a particular matter that indicates the person needs coaching in "next steps"; that is, specific feedback about the matter.

For example, you might focus on the performance of a specific task. (If you also chose this person for the Accuracy exercise in Chapter 5, you can focus on the same issue you did there, or on a new one.)

Please record the issue in the appropriate space on the worksheet.

4 Clarify your purpose in terms as specific as you can make them. What tangible result do you hope to achieve by giving the feedback?

Please record your purpose in the appropriate space on the worksheet.

(Steps continued after worksheet) ➡

Exercise 3 — Worksheet

FEEDBACK RECIPIENT: _____
(Direct Report/Valued Co-Worker)

THE PERFORMANCE MATTER UNDER FOCUS

CLARIFYING YOUR PURPOSE
What tangible results do you hope to achieve through the feedback?

PREPARING YOUR FEEDBACK (COACHING "NEXT STEPS")

TANGIBLE GOALS	GOAL DEADLINES	PARAMETERS, GUIDELINES

➡
Go on to next page

Exercise 3 — Worksheet (concluded)

PREPARING YOUR FEEDBACK (Continue list as needed.)

TANGIBLE GOALS	GOAL DEADLINES	PARAMETERS, GUIDELINES

REFINING THE MESSAGE

➡ **EXERCISE 3: GIVING SPECIFIC FEEDBACK**

5 Assign concrete actions based on the tangible results you
hope to achieve.

This step requires that you do the following:

- Delegate clear tangible goals
- Assign goal deadlines
- Spell out upfront any guidelines and parameters

*Please record these goals, deadlines, and parameters in the
appropriate columns of the accompanying worksheet.*

6 Refine your feedback message before delivering it.

You may even want to rehearse the message verbally.
This will give you a better sense of just how clear your
feedback message really is, and alert you to areas that
require further refinement.

*If you wish, refine your message in writing, using the
appropriate space on the accompanying worksheet.*

**Whenever you need to give someone feedback,
return to this exercise for preparation.**

CONCLUDED ●

FAST Tips . . . for Making Feedback More Specific

Here are some FAST tips that will help you ensure your feedback is *specific.* Use the space that concludes this chapter to add your own suggestions.

1. Always clarify the purpose of your feedback before giving it.

2. Link feedback directly to concrete action steps.

3. If you are giving feedback about process, make sure to clearly explain the feedback's impact on results. (Answer the question: "Why does it matter *how* I do it as long as it gets done?")

4. Evaluate the performance, not the person.

5. Provide relevant details (who, what, where, why, when, how).

6. Tell employees exactly what they do right and exactly what they need to improve.

7. If the concrete action steps you are assigning require tasks that are new to the employee, provide a model that he or she can imitate.

8. Never give the employee dirty looks, and never go with the "you're in the doghouse" approach; extreme expressions of disapproval damage

employee morale and rarely improve performance.

9. Always tie pats on the back (praise) to *particular* instances of performance, and mention the details; broad expressions of approval are not much better than extreme expressions of disapproval.

10. In the case of "big picture" feedback, give examples of particular instances of performance; include details and have documentation available to support your case.

YOUR OWN FAST TIPS:

☰ Chapter 7 ☰

TIMELY FEEDBACK
The Sooner, The Better

THE FOURTH KEY to the FAST approach is giving feedback that is timely. This is also the fourth key behavior of the best coaching-style managers, according to our extensive research.

The Importance of Timely Feedback

The *Timely* element of FAST Feedback is integral to feedback that makes a strong impact on the employee and job performance. When feedback is immediate, the employee's recall is at an optimum, the context of the feedback is evident, and the significance of the performance in question can be

> ⑉➡ *Remember . . .*
> **Timely feedback ensures employees receive feedback soon enough for it to have an impact on performance.**

readily appreciated. The result is effective feedback—the kind that leads to performance improvement.

> ## ▲ Why Immediate Feedback Makes the Greatest Impact
>
> 1. *Employee recall is at an optimum.*
>
> 2. *The context of the feedback is evident.*
>
> 3. *The significance of the performance in question can readily be appreciated.*

With each moment that passes between an employee's performance and a manager's feedback, the feedback loses impact. Remember: very few people recollect with precision every action they take, every word they utter or write, and every result they achieve. That's why it's not unusual for an employee to respond to delayed feedback by thinking or saying, "What are you talking about?"

Remember, too: employees perform all day long, day after day, week after week. The more distant in time the performance being evaluated, the more like ancient history the performance will seem. An employee is apt to think, "Why didn't you mention it at the time?"

What is more, elapsed time is likely to diminish the apparent significance of the performance, leading the employee to wonder, "Why are you bothering me about such a trivial matter?"

THE IMPACT ON TURNAROUND TIME

The timeliness of a manager's feedback also has a substantial impact on the turnaround time of an employee's work product. That's because employees usually seek feedback when they hit a natural stopping point. This may be a final result, an intermediate step in a work in progress, an unresolved question or problem, or a need for approval of some kind.

Whatever the stopping point, by seeking your feedback, the employee is placing the ball in your court. (William Onken would say, "The employee is placing the monkey on your back.") Until you respond, no work will get done on the matter in question. You must accelerate the turnaround time, and keep the ball in play (get the monkey off your back).

THE NECESSITY OF TIMELY FEEDBACK

There are many reasons why timely feedback is such a necessity in today's workplace. Prominent among those reasons are the following:

1. **Timely feedback allows time for action.** When feedback is given soon after the performance in question, both the manager and the employee have sufficient time to take action if action is warranted. Assuming the feedback points to concrete action steps (is specific), the manager

must give the employee enough time to do all of the following:

▲ Accept 100 percent responsibility for those action steps

▲ Understand and follow guidelines and parameters

▲ Agree on a time frame

▲ Achieve the assigned tangible results by a reasonable deadline

2. **Timely feedback optimizes employee learning opportunities.** Employees learn best from feedback that resonates with a recent experience, is still relevant to their current work, and can still be applied in a way that provides reinforcement.

3. **Timely feedback fits the demands of today's workplace.** Managers and employees alike must keep up with the rapid pace of the new JUSTinTIME workplace, and timely feedback helps them do it.

TIMELY AND FREQUENT: DISTINCTIONS

It should be noted that timeliness is different from, though related to, frequency. As we saw in Chapter 4, every employee has his or her unique frequency—that is, "the number of opportunities for feedback produced

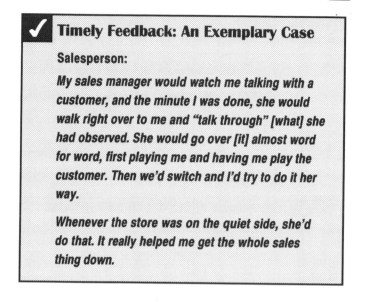

> ✓ **Timely Feedback: An Exemplary Case**
>
> **Salesperson:**
>
> *My sales manager would watch me talking with a customer, and the minute I was done, she would walk right over to me and "talk through" [what] she had observed. She would go over [it] almost word for word, first playing me and having me play the customer. Then we'd switch and I'd try to do it her way.*
>
> *Whenever the store was on the quiet side, she'd do that. It really helped me get the whole sales thing down.*

by the employee's performance." Timeliness is about seizing those opportunities immediately, as they present themselves. In practice, frequency requires the manager to pay close attention to how much feedback an employee needs. Timeliness almost always comes down to the manager's time-management skills.

UNTIMELY FEEDBACK: THE TOP FIVE CAUSES

Our research has revealed five major causes of untimely feedback. They are presented next and followed by guidelines that will help ensure that your feedback is timely and effective.

OUR RESEARCH REVEALS...

UNTIMELY FEEDBACK
The Top Five Causes

1. The manager feels too busy with other tasks and responsibilities, and so fails to make immediate feedback a priority.

2. The manager considers immediate feedback a priority, but lacks the time-management skills needed to act on that priority.

3. The manager waits for a "good time" to give the feedback, and so misses the best time (right away).

4. The manager does not give immediate feedback because of anxiety about its potential consequences (such as discomfort, anger, hurt feelings, losing a valued employee).

5. The manager relies too much on the formal review process.

GUIDELINES

Giving Timely Feedback

1.
Always remember that immediate feedback makes the greatest impact.

The performance details are fresh and clear, the context is evident, and the significance of the performance is more readily appreciated.

2.
Make time right away for feedback and save time later.

Immediate feedback is like an ounce of prevention: it will save you tons of trouble in the future. Resist the temptation to wait for a "good time" to give feedback, because the longer you wait, the more likely it is that a "good time" won't come until you must step in to put out fires and handle damage control.

3.
Develop good time-management skills.

Try to predict when feedback will be required. The more you can anticipate, the more you'll be able to plan ahead. In cases where you can't plan ahead, stop and plan on the spot: schedule a precise block of time for today, tomorrow, or at least this week, to deliver feedback.

➥

➡ GUIDELINES
Giving Timely Feedback

4. **Be brief and simple.**
As long as you take the time upfront to check
for accuracy and create a specific script, you
will be on your way to brevity and simplicity.
The final key is making sure you achieve
brevity and simplicity in your actual delivery.
Once again, that means *stick to the script.*

CONCLUDED ●

EXERCISE 4: Giving Timely Feedback

The following two-part exercise will help you anticipate the need for feedback and make time for feedback
in your weekly schedule. Note the inclusion of two
worksheets, which make completion easier and reinforce learning. Return to this exercise whenever you
feel you are getting too busy to provide direct reports
and other valued co-workers with timely feedback.

☛ **Please note that an additional copy of this
exercise can be found in Appendix C.**

EXERCISE 4:
GIVING TIMELY FEEDBACK
Anticipating Feedback and Making Time for It

PART 1 Anticipating the Need for Feedback

1 Take a moment to think about the direct reports and other valued co-workers you manage. Which ones do you think will require feedback in the week ahead? Now *record their names in the left-hand column of Worksheet A.*

2 For each person you listed, anticipate the performance matters that will likely require feedback. (Consider final results, intermediate results, works in progress, and other instances of performance.)

Please record each matter in the center column of Worksheet A, next to the name of the direct report/co-worker.

3 For each matter, estimate the day (and, if possible, time) that the feedback will be required.

Please record estimations in the right-hand column of Worksheet A, next to their corresponding matter.

PART 2 Your Weekly Schedule: Making Time for Feedback

1 If you have your day planner or calendar with you, please take it out and review the week ahead.

(Step 1 continued after worksheets) ➡

Exercise 4 — Worksheet A

WHO WILL NEED FEEDBACK? (Please list.)	WHAT MATTERS WILL REQUIRE FEEDBACK? (Please list.)	WHEN? (Please list day and time.)
	))))➡	))))➡
	))))➡	))))➡
	))))➡	))))➡
	))))➡	))))➡
	))))➡	))))➡
	))))➡	))))➡
	))))➡	))))➡
	))))➡	))))➡

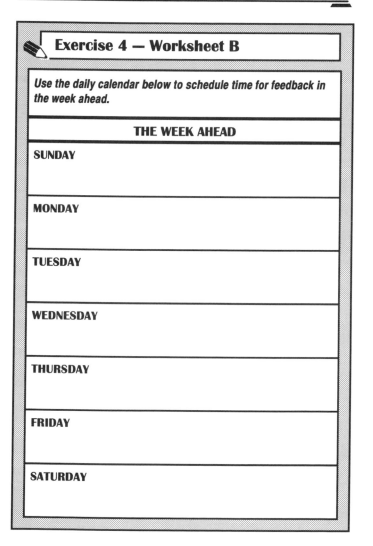

Exercise 4 — Worksheet B

Use the daily calendar below to schedule time for feedback in the week ahead.

THE WEEK AHEAD
SUNDAY
MONDAY
TUESDAY
WEDNESDAY
THURSDAY
FRIDAY
SATURDAY

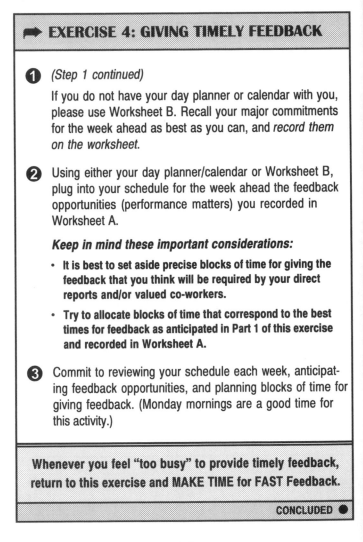

➡ EXERCISE 4: GIVING TIMELY FEEDBACK

❶ *(Step 1 continued)*

If you do not have your day planner or calendar with you, please use Worksheet B. Recall your major commitments for the week ahead as best as you can, and *record them on the worksheet.*

❷ Using either your day planner/calendar or Worksheet B, plug into your schedule for the week ahead the feedback opportunities (performance matters) you recorded in Worksheet A.

Keep in mind these important considerations:

- **It is best to set aside precise blocks of time for giving the feedback that you think will be required by your direct reports and/or valued co-workers.**

- **Try to allocate blocks of time that correspond to the best times for feedback as anticipated in Part 1 of this exercise and recorded in Worksheet A.**

❸ Commit to reviewing your schedule each week, anticipating feedback opportunities, and planning blocks of time for giving feedback. (Monday mornings are a good time for this activity.)

Whenever you feel "too busy" to provide timely feedback, return to this exercise and MAKE TIME for FAST Feedback.

CONCLUDED ●

FAST Tips . . . for Giving Timely Feedback

Here are some FAST tips that will help ensure your feedback is immediate and effective. Use the space that concludes this chapter to add your own suggestions.

1. Try to anticipate upcoming feedback opportunities (relevant inputs from employees), and plan time in your schedule to act on them.

2. Give yourself regular deadlines for providing feedback, and stick to those deadlines.

3. Give yourself a 48-hour rule for giving feedback on any employee work in progress.

4. Block out a regular time every day or every week for providing feedback. During these times, identify the best feedback opportunities and seize them. (Note: this strategy is particularly good for managers who have many direct reports.)

5. Provide on-the-spot feedback whenever the opportunity arises. (However, don't neglect the other FAST elements: be sure to take a moment to reflect on the situation, clarify your purpose, balance praise and criticism, define concrete action steps, and rehearse feedback delivery.)

6. Use the time for feedback interaction wisely. Get right to the point—be as brief as possible while still conveying your *entire* message clearly. This will minimize time costs and interruptions to your work flow.

7. Provide feedback in a form that is convenient for you—voice-mail, e-mail, brief notes. (However, don't neglect to consider the form of feedback that will be most effective with the recipient.)

8. Create a standard process for employee feedback requests, and reward employees when they use that process to ask for feedback.

9. Develop resources such as standardized memo templates (see Appendix D), and use them to make it easier and less time-consuming to give immediate feedback that is accurate and specific.

10. Shift some non-feedback tasks to times when you do not have opportunities for direct contact with your employees.

11. Reward employees for good judgment and timing in their feedback requests.

12. Give employees feedback in a form and a manner that improve their ability to process the feedback quickly.

13. Conduct an overall time-management self-assessment, and remove time-wasters and interruptions.

YOUR OWN FAST TIPS:

≡ Chapter 8 ≡

WHY TURN MANAGERS INTO COACHES?

COACHING-STYLE MANAGEMENT has always been the most effective approach to developing people's talents, but in the new workplace, it is *a business imperative.* Today's employers need flexible workers, ones who are prepared to adapt to rapidly changing circumstances and *get the job done,* whatever the job may be on any given day. That's why the most valuable workers today are entrepreneurial, technoliterate, and results-focused individuals who

> ⟫⟫ *Remember . . .*
>
> **FAST Feedback is based on the best practices of the best coaching-style managers. By taking the FAST approach, any manager can develop and bring out the effective coach within.**

are always seeking new opportunities, ready to adapt to new situations, and passionate about their personal and professional growth. Coaching-style management supports and empowers in such workers the highest levels of personal responsibility, self-management, initiative, and motivation. It also helps employees, in general, develop along these lines of value. As a result, the entire organization benefits.

The Power of Coaching-Style Management

To bring out the best in the best people today, and to foster the potential for the best in others, managers must develop the skills that coaching-style managers regularly exhibit. These skills enable managers to:

▲ Build trust with the people they supervise

▲ Make meaningful connections with employees on a routine basis

▲ Mentor employees—give them encouragement, push them to higher levels, and offer guidance along the path of continual improvement

The payoffs include a number of results essential to success, including:

▲ *Efficient, hard-working employees who give the organization the competitive edge*

▲ *Productivity in a fluid labor market*

▲ *The right balance between employee empowerment and managerial guidance*

▲ *Maintenance of the competitive advantage*

THE COMPETITIVE EDGE

Coaching-style managers are consistently the ones with the high-performing teams in terms of morale, productivity, quality, and retention.

They are the leaders for whom employees will work *the hardest, the best, the fastest*— and go the extra mile. In today's fiercely competitive global economy, employees like these are often the key to seizing market opportunities before

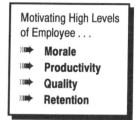

Motivating High Levels of Employee . . .
⟫ **Morale**
⟫ **Productivity**
⟫ **Quality**
⟫ **Retention**

they disappear, beating competitors to the marketplace, and achieving rapid turnaround rates on products and services.

PRODUCTIVITY IN A FLUID LABOR MARKET

Coaching-style managers are also equipped to handle the complications of today's

fluid labor market. So many of the most valuable workers are in constant motion—just passing through companies, working one- to three-year tours of duty; operating as independent contractors, temps, or

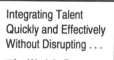

Integrating Talent Quickly and Effectively Without Disrupting . . .
⟫ Work in Progress
⟫ Core Employees

consultants; or serving on an outsourcing basis. With more and more people working in organizations under their own "special" arrangements, managers need to integrate talent quickly and effectively on an ongoing basis without disrupting work in progress and the longer-term core-group employees.

Those who practice coaching-style management have a distinct advantage when it comes to these challenges. They know how to tune in to each employee's unique frequency and keep each person focused, motivated, and moving in the right direction—despite the environment of constant change.

THE RIGHT BALANCE OF EMPOWERMENT AND GUIDANCE

Simply telling employees "We want you to treat this project like your own little business" is not enough to strike the right balance between employee empowerment and manager guidance. More than ever

> Communicating to Employees . . .
> ⮕ Responsibility
> ⮕ Accountability
> ⮕ Expected Results

before, organizations need managers who know how to make clear exactly where each person's responsibility begins and ends. Managers must be able to communicate effectively where each person's creative freedom begins and ends, the tangible results for which each person will be held accountable, and what results each person must achieve to receive credit and rewards.

MAINTENANCE OF THE COMPETITIVE ADVANTAGE

In the new JUSTinTIME business world, coaching-style managers are absolutely necessary to the competitive advantage that comes from consistently motivating and retaining the best workers. These managers are so effective because coaching is, in itself, a process geared to more than a single win in a single instance: it is geared to *solid achievement*—to developing and maintaining the conditions for *long-term success.* Coaching-style managers achieve results by:

> Using Coaching-Style Management to Generate Short-Term *and* Long-Term Success

▲ Getting employees up to speed quickly so they can start adding value right away

▲ Helping employees anticipate knowledge and skill gaps and other learning needs on an ongoing basis

▲ Making sure employees have access to the right learning resources at the right time

▲ Building credibility so they can work with employees regularly on . . .

— personal effectiveness

— career planning and professional development

— leveraging information, skill, and knowledge routinely in daily tasks and responsibilities

Such managers stay in constant touch with employees, watching for "red flags" that signal unnecessary turnover. They build personal retention plans each day with their most valuable direct reports; when necessary they help the best employees find internal "escape hatches" by moving them around the organization into new skill areas, new projects, new locations, new teams, or new work schedules.

Profound Change — and Crucial Need

Nowadays it seems that everyone is remapping the way to success, trying to find the best course of action for navigating through the most profound economic changes since the Industrial Revolution. Technology, globalization, and the accelerating pace of change have yielded chaotic markets, fierce competition, and unpredictable staffing needs, impelling business leaders to turn the traditional model of work on its head. Downsizing, restructuring, and reengineering have fundamentally reshaped the nature of work and radically altered the employer–employee relationship. Skilled workers now trade security for mobility, and more and more consider themselves "free agents."

With the revised model of work, and the free-agent workforce charting a whole new career path, many traditional management strategies have become obsolete. Managers might still rely on them, feeling there are no alternatives, but few can reasonably expect employees to be motivated by prospects of long-term employment and progression up the organization hierarchy: both are remnants of the past. And six-month reviews, annual raises, and other traditional rewards and incentives no longer have the impact they once had.

However, there is one tried-and-true management strategy that fits the workplace of today even better than it did the workplace of the past: day-to-day coaching-style management. Today this strategy is a business *imperative* because it is in perfect sync with the needs of the new free-agent career path *and* the dynamics of the new JUSTinTIME workplace.

Organizations that adopt this strategy, and insist on turning every manager into a coach, can get a handle on change and successfully make it work for them. They will lead the competition in the economy of the future because they will be able to:

▲ Recruit the best people and get the desired return on their recruiting and training investments

▲ Handle workplace changes with flexibility and dexterity

▲ Become centers of innovation and new value creation

Coaching-style management fulfills a crucial, multi-faceted organizational need in the new economy. Time

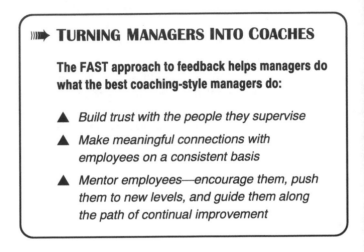

》》》➡ **TURNING MANAGERS INTO COACHES**

The FAST approach to feedback helps managers do what the best coaching-style managers do:

▲ *Build trust with the people they supervise*

▲ *Make meaningful connections with employees on a consistent basis*

▲ *Mentor employees—encourage them, push them to new levels, and guide them along the path of continual improvement*

will only intensify this need, too, for in essence the workplace of today no longer straddles the past and the the future: it *is* the future.

Finding Your Inner Coach With *FAST Feedback*

As you have learned in this book, the best coaching-style managers have something very important in common: they give employees FAST Feedback. If you are not practicing FAST Feedback already, begin today and transform your role as a manager and your relationships with the people you manage. There is a great coach inside you. FAST Feedback will bring out that great coach and put that coach into action.

Chapter 9

ONE LAST FAST REVIEW

I WOULD LIKE TO REPEAT one final time that FAST Feedback is a system which encapsulates the best practices of the best coaching-style managers—those who know how to keep individual performers focused and motivated day after day—based on the ongoing workplace-interview research conducted by RainmakerThinking. I would also like to review with you one more time some of the most important points about FAST Feedback.

Reviewing the FAST Approach

Fundamental to FAST Feedback is the emphasis on feedback itself, which is, by definition, a *responsive* form of communication. Coaching is an ongoing series of *responses* to someone's performance. *Giving feedback* is the core competency of every coach. According to our research, the FASTer the feedback, the better the coach.

>>> **F** requent
>>> **A** ccurate
>>> **S** pecific
>>> **T** imely

THE MANY POSITIVE RESULTS OF FAST FEEDBACK

Our approach to feedback is designed to help anyone in a position of supervisory responsibility contribute to such active improvements as:

- ▲ Providing employees with regular guidance as needed
- ▲ Giving employees a greater feeling of being "in the loop"
- ▲ Building managers' credibility with employees
- ▲ Increasing the quality of manager–employee interactions
- ▲ Making responsive coaching the centerpiece of supervisory relationships
- ▲ Encouraging ongoing results-oriented dialogues between managers and employees
- ▲ Enabling responsible delegation through regular, built-in review and revision
- ▲ Linking performance evaluation directly to concrete action steps
- ▲ Separating performance evaluation from annual raises and promotions
- ▲ Accelerating turnaround time and increasing productivity

Reviewing the Four Elements of FAST Feedback

 **FREQUENT**   Some employees need feedback
more often than others—each person has a unique "feedback frequency" rate, and differs in the number of feedback opportunities produced by his or her work performance. Giving different employees feedback at their unique rates of need is the first key behavior of the best coaching-style managers. *Identifying and tuning in to each employee's frequency* is the corresponding skill.

FREQUENT FEEDBACK: GUIDELINES

1. Recognize every employee's unique frequency.

2. Note that tasks and responsibilities yield feedback opportunities.

3. Tune in to feedback opportunities.

4. When in doubt, give feedback; then pay close attention to the result.

ACCURATE   Every instance of feedback has an effect on the employee's trust and performance. Giving feedback that is correct, balanced, and appropriate is the second key behavior of the best coaching-style managers. Its corresponding skill includes *taking the time to reflect, question assumptions, check facts, and rehearse the feedback's delivery.*

ACCURATE FEEDBACK: GUIDELINES

1. Remember, your credibility is on the line.
2. In preparing to give feedback, stop and reflect on the content of the feedback.
3. Balance praise and criticism.
4. Refine your message and rehearse.

 **SPECIFIC** Telling people exactly what they do right and wrong is not specific enough—you must also tell people exactly what next steps are necessary to achieve the best results. This is the third key behavior, with *setting concrete goals and deadlines, and providing clear guidelines,* as the corresponding skill.

SPECIFIC FEEDBACK: GUIDELINES

1. Look at evaluation as a chance for action.
2. Clarify your exact purpose for giving the feedback.
3. Next, assign concrete action steps.
4. Finally, get some feedback on your feedback.

▒▒▶ **TIMELY**   The closer in time feedback follows the performance in question, the more impact it will have on the employee, and the better the chances that any needed improvements will be made. Giving feedback immediately is thus the fourth key behavior of good coaching-style managers. *Effective time management* is its corresponding skill.

TIMELY FEEDBACK: GUIDELINES

1. Always remember that immediate feedback makes the greatest impact.

2. Make time right away for feedback and save time later.

3. Develop good time-management skills.

4. Be brief and simple.

In Conclusion . . .

It is my great hope that as you read this second edition of FAST Feedback, you kept at the forefront of your mind the direct reports and valued co-workers you work with most closely. In the end, FAST Feedback is about nothing if it is not about your day-to-day relationships with these people.

As soon as you begin practicing FAST Feedback, you will see a difference in your relationships with the people you manage. If every manager in your organization is trained in the FAST Feedback method and the approach is widely implemented, it will change the role of managers and fundamentally improve the relationship between them and employees. And once a critical mass of your managers begins practicing FAST Feedback, this behavior change will create a dynamic environment of results-oriented dialogue, constant learning, high trust, increased productivity, accelerated turnaround time, improved morale, and lower turnover.

If you are not practicing FAST Feedback already, I hope the second edition of this pocket guide has given you the tools you need to begin today.

APPENDICES

≡ Appendix A ≡≡≡≡≡

FAST FEEDBACK TRAINING AND IMPLEMENTATION

OUR INTERVIEW RESEARCH AT RAINMAKERTHINKING is an ongoing effort to gather and analyze the invaluable data that people at the front lines of the workplace have to offer. Working with such data, we have developed a four-hour licensable training program to teach managers the fundamental behaviors and skills of FAST Feedback. The program, *FAST Feedback: Coaching Skills for Managers,*

> Bring FAST to Your Workplace With . . .
>
> **The FAST Feedback Training Program**
>
> **COACHING SKILLS FOR MANAGERS**

focuses on building the four key behaviors and corresponding skills practiced by the most effective managers—the ones our interviewees regarded as "the best [they've] ever had." The program is intended to teach anyone in a position of supervisory responsibility how to bring out the best in the people they manage and coach employees to success in the fast-paced workplace of the future.

TRAINING AND IMPLEMENTATION: WHAT THEY CAN DO FOR YOUR ORGANIZATION

If every manager with supervisory responsibility is trained in the FAST approach, and if the approach is widely implemented in your organization, you should see positive changes in these and other areas:

▲ **Organizational Behavior.** FAST Feedback will change the role of managers in your organization and transform the relationship between managers and the people they supervise. This change will create a dynamic environment of results-oriented dialogue, constant learning, high trust, increased productivity, accelerated turnaround time, improved morale, and lower turnover.

▲ **Management Style.** Every manager who starts practicing FAST Feedback will be on the path to effective *coaching-style management,* thus supporting and adding to the dramatic improvements mentioned above.

▲ **Team Communication.** FAST Feedback will energize interactions between and among team members. It will speed up and simplify internal

queries, information sharing, assignment split-
ting, collaboration, assessment, revision, and
project news.

MAXIMIZING THE BENEFITS

You can increase the benefits above by using FAST
Feedback for:

▲ **Performance Evaluation.** Managers will find
they can use FAST Feedback in place of other
evaluation systems, or in conjunction with them,
to track employee performance and conduct
developmental needs assessment on a regular
basis.

▲ **360° FAST Feedback.** FAST Feedback is not
just for feedback from managers to employees.
The same approach can be applied to lateral and
upward evaluation, communication, and coaching.

DIFFERENT APPROACHES TO FAST IMPLEMENTATION

You can use FAST Feedback in various formats and for a
wide assortment of purposes, including the following:

▲ **Formal, Large-Scale Change.** By training
every manager in FAST Feedback and implementing the approach on a large scale, you can
facilitate an overall corporate culture shift. The
many benefits of FAST Feedback will transform

your corporate culture and head it in the direction of solid, long-lasting success.

▲ **Informal Change.** You do not have to implement FAST Feedback formally for it to make an impact on your organization. If organizational leaders commit to the FAST philosophy, they can spread the message on many levels. As the message spreads, shrewd managers and other leaders will begin using FAST Feedback, and their success will inspire others.

▲ **Team Meetings.** Organizational leaders can use FAST Feedback to improve communication at team meetings and provide members with the responsive communication and guidance they need.

▲ **One-on-One.** Even one leader providing FAST Feedback to one employee will have an impact, at least on that one employee.

▲ **Voice-mail or E-mail.** With minimal time and effort, managers can deliver FAST Feedback messages daily by voice-mail or e-mail.

▲ **The Paper Trail.** You can use FAST Feedback in place of, or to supplement, traditional six- and twelve-month reviews. (Keep in mind: you may need to develop a written format and create a system for recording such written exchanges.)

THE FAST FEEDBACK TRAINING PROGRAM
COACHING SKILLS FOR MANAGERS

The FAST behaviors and skills are taught in a four-hour program through a combination of video, leader presentation, group interaction, and individual exercises. The materials for the program are shown below.

PARTICIPANT MATERIALS

- ⟫ **Participant Workbook**

- ⟫ *FAST Feedback,* **Second Edition**

- ⟫ **The FAST Feedback Manager's Tool Kit**
  This kit contains useful tools from the program to help participants apply the FAST methodology. (Available in print and electronic form.)

- ⟫ **FAST Feedback Wallet Card**

TRAINER MATERIALS

- ⟫ **Leader's Guide**

- ⟫ *FAST Feedback,* **Second Edition**

➡

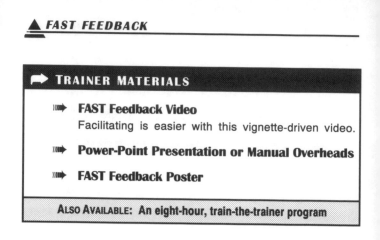

➡ **TRAINER MATERIALS**

⟫➤ **FAST Feedback Video**
Facilitating is easier with this vignette-driven video.

⟫➤ **Power-Point Presentation or Manual Overheads**

⟫➤ **FAST Feedback Poster**

ALSO AVAILABLE: An eight-hour, train-the-trainer program

For more information on implementing FAST Feedback
in your organization, contact
RainmakerThinking at **203-772-2002.**

For information on ordering FAST Feedback materials,
contact **HRD Press** at **1-800-822-2801.**

The FAST Evaluations

1. **FAST FEEDBACK SELF-EVALUATION**
   Identifying Your Strengths and Weakesses

2. **FAST FEEDBACK EVALUATION (OTHER)**
   Assessing Your Manager's Feedback

☞ *For background information on the*
FAST evaluations, please see Chapter 3.

1 FAST Feedback Self-Evaluation

FAST FEEDBACK SELF-EVALUATION
Identifying Your Strengths and Weaknesses

STEP 1. RECALLING YOUR FEEDBACK INTERACTION

Please select a direct report or other valued co-worker for your focus here. (If you made a list of direct reports and valued co-workers earlier, in the Introduction, return to the list and choose someone).

Now recall the last time you communicated with this person about his or her performance. Try to remember as many details of the communication as you can. You may recall more details if you make notes about the episode using the work space below.

WORK SPACE

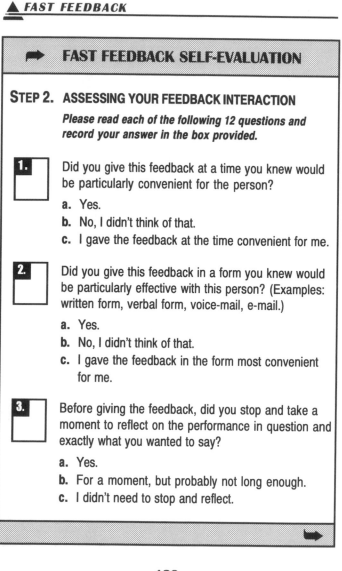

➡ **FAST FEEDBACK SELF-EVALUATION**

STEP 2. **ASSESSING YOUR FEEDBACK INTERACTION**

Please read each of the following 12 questions and record your answer in the box provided.

1. Did you give this feedback at a time you knew would be particularly convenient for the person?

a. Yes.
b. No, I didn't think of that.
c. I gave the feedback at the time convenient for me.

2. Did you give this feedback in a form you knew would be particularly effective with this person? (Examples: written form, verbal form, voice-mail, e-mail.)

a. Yes.
b. No, I didn't think of that.
c. I gave the feedback in the form most convenient for me.

3. Before giving the feedback, did you stop and take a moment to reflect on the performance in question and exactly what you wanted to say?

a. Yes.
b. For a moment, but probably not long enough.
c. I didn't need to stop and reflect.

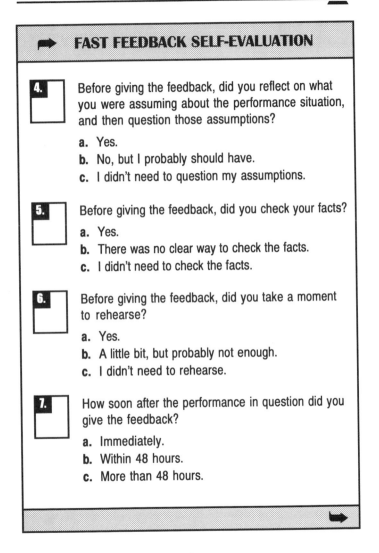

➡ FAST FEEDBACK SELF-EVALUATION

4. Before giving the feedback, did you reflect on what you were assuming about the performance situation, and then question those assumptions?

a. Yes.
b. No, but I probably should have.
c. I didn't need to question my assumptions.

5. Before giving the feedback, did you check your facts?

a. Yes.
b. There was no clear way to check the facts.
c. I didn't need to check the facts.

6. Before giving the feedback, did you take a moment to rehearse?

a. Yes.
b. A little bit, but probably not enough.
c. I didn't need to rehearse.

7. How soon after the performance in question did you give the feedback?

a. Immediately.
b. Within 48 hours.
c. More than 48 hours.

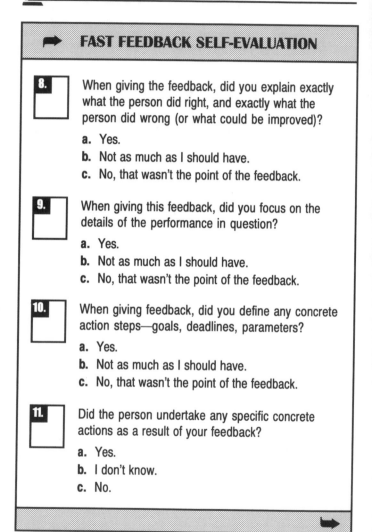

➡ **FAST FEEDBACK SELF-EVALUATION**

8. When giving the feedback, did you explain exactly what the person did right, and exactly what the person did wrong (or what could be improved)?

a. Yes.
b. Not as much as I should have.
c. No, that wasn't the point of the feedback.

9. When giving this feedback, did you focus on the details of the performance in question?

a. Yes.
b. Not as much as I should have.
c. No, that wasn't the point of the feedback.

10. When giving feedback, did you define any concrete action steps—goals, deadlines, parameters?

a. Yes.
b. Not as much as I should have.
c. No, that wasn't the point of the feedback.

11. Did the person undertake any specific concrete actions as a result of your feedback?

a. Yes.
b. I don't know.
c. No.

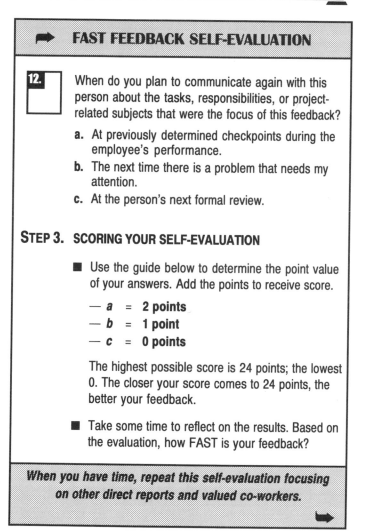

➡ FAST FEEDBACK SELF-EVALUATION

12. When do you plan to communicate again with this person about the tasks, responsibilities, or project-related subjects that were the focus of this feedback?

a. At previously determined checkpoints during the employee's performance.

b. The next time there is a problem that needs my attention.

c. At the person's next formal review.

STEP 3. SCORING YOUR SELF-EVALUATION

■ Use the guide below to determine the point value of your answers. Add the points to receive score.

— *a* = **2 points**
— *b* = **1 point**
— *c* = **0 points**

The highest possible score is 24 points; the lowest 0. The closer your score comes to 24 points, the better your feedback.

■ Take some time to reflect on the results. Based on the evaluation, how FAST is your feedback?

When you have time, repeat this self-evaluation focusing on other direct reports and valued co-workers.

➡

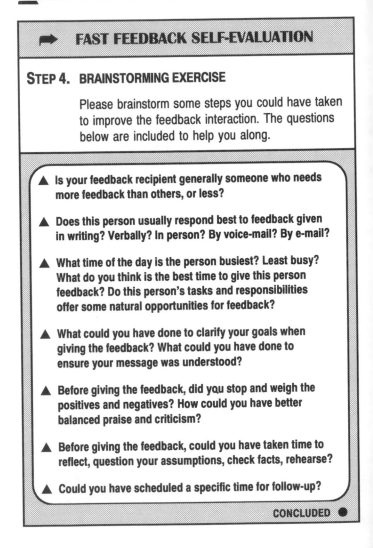

➡ **FAST FEEDBACK SELF-EVALUATION**

STEP 4. **BRAINSTORMING EXERCISE**

Please brainstorm some steps you could have taken to improve the feedback interaction. The questions below are included to help you along.

▲ Is your feedback recipient generally someone who needs more feedback than others, or less?

▲ Does this person usually respond best to feedback given in writing? Verbally? In person? By voice-mail? By e-mail?

▲ What time of the day is the person busiest? Least busy? What do you think is the best time to give this person feedback? Do this person's tasks and responsibilities offer some natural opportunities for feedback?

▲ What could you have done to clarify your goals when giving the feedback? What could you have done to ensure your message was understood?

▲ Before giving the feedback, did you stop and weigh the positives and negatives? How could you have better balanced praise and criticism?

▲ Before giving the feedback, could you have taken time to reflect, question your assumptions, check facts, rehearse?

▲ Could you have scheduled a specific time for follow-up?

CONCLUDED ●

2 FAST Feedback Evaluation (Other)

FAST FEEDBACK EVALUATION
Assessing Your Manager's Feedback

STEP 1. RECALLING FEEDBACK YOU RECEIVED

Take a moment to think of a senior manager you report to now or a manager you have reported to in the past.

Now recall a time when you were on the receiving end of that manager's feedback—a time when he or she communicated with you about your performance. Try to recall as many details of the communication as you can. Make notes in the work space below if it will help you remember the feedback episode better.

WORK SPACE

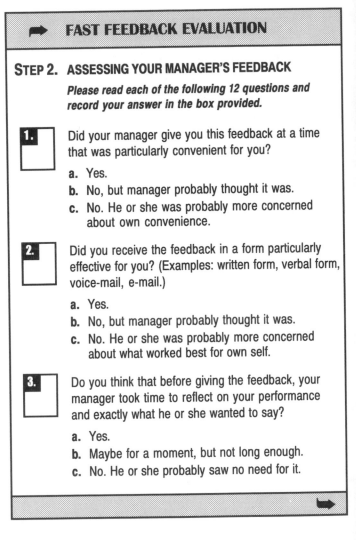

➡️ **FAST FEEDBACK EVALUATION**

STEP 2. **ASSESSING YOUR MANAGER'S FEEDBACK**

Please read each of the following 12 questions and record your answer in the box provided.

1. Did your manager give you this feedback at a time that was particularly convenient for you?

   a. Yes.

   b. No, but manager probably thought it was.

   c. No. He or she was probably more concerned about own convenience.

2. Did you receive the feedback in a form particularly effective for you? (Examples: written form, verbal form, voice-mail, e-mail.)

   a. Yes.

   b. No, but manager probably thought it was.

   c. No. He or she was probably more concerned about what worked best for own self.

3. Do you think that before giving the feedback, your manager took time to reflect on your performance and exactly what he or she wanted to say?

   a. Yes.

   b. Maybe for a moment, but not long enough.

   c. No. He or she probably saw no need for it.

➡️

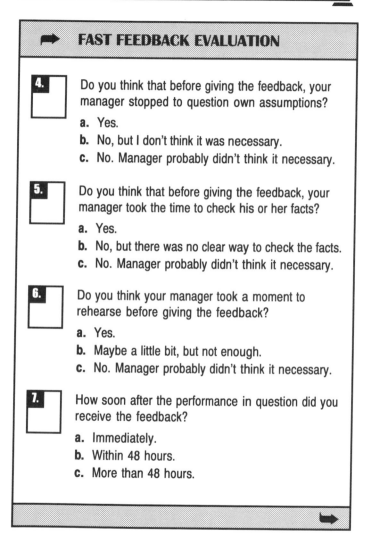

➡ FAST FEEDBACK EVALUATION

4.
Do you think that before giving the feedback, your manager stopped to question own assumptions?

a. Yes.
b. No, but I don't think it was necessary.
c. No. Manager probably didn't think it necessary.

5.
Do you think that before giving the feedback, your manager took the time to check his or her facts?

a. Yes.
b. No, but there was no clear way to check the facts.
c. No. Manager probably didn't think it necessary.

6.
Do you think your manager took a moment to rehearse before giving the feedback?

a. Yes.
b. Maybe a little bit, but not enough.
c. No. Manager probably didn't think it necessary.

7.
How soon after the performance in question did you receive the feedback?

a. Immediately.
b. Within 48 hours.
c. More than 48 hours.

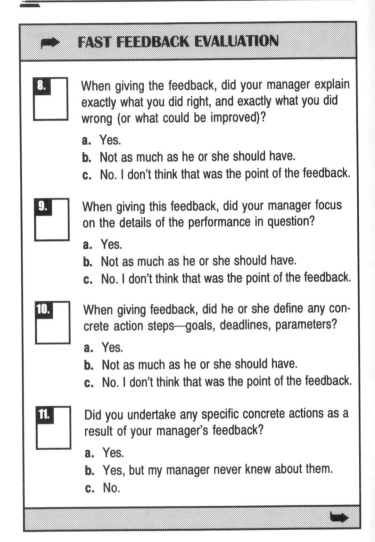

➡ **FAST FEEDBACK EVALUATION**

8. When giving the feedback, did your manager explain exactly what you did right, and exactly what you did wrong (or what could be improved)?

a. Yes.
b. Not as much as he or she should have.
c. No. I don't think that was the point of the feedback.

9. When giving this feedback, did your manager focus on the details of the performance in question?

a. Yes.
b. Not as much as he or she should have.
c. No. I don't think that was the point of the feedback.

10. When giving feedback, did he or she define any concrete action steps—goals, deadlines, parameters?

a. Yes.
b. Not as much as he or she should have.
c. No. I don't think that was the point of the feedback.

11. Did you undertake any specific concrete actions as a result of your manager's feedback?

a. Yes.
b. Yes, but my manager never knew about them.
c. No.

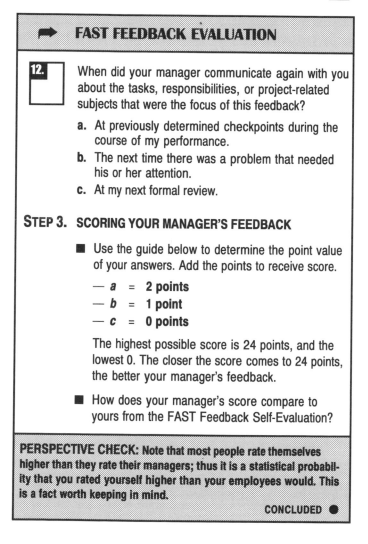

➡ **FAST FEEDBACK EVALUATION**

12. When did your manager communicate again with you about the tasks, responsibilities, or project-related subjects that were the focus of this feedback?

a. At previously determined checkpoints during the course of my performance.

b. The next time there was a problem that needed his or her attention.

c. At my next formal review.

STEP 3. SCORING YOUR MANAGER'S FEEDBACK

■ Use the guide below to determine the point value of your answers. Add the points to receive score.

— *a* = **2 points**
— *b* = **1 point**
— *c* = **0 points**

The highest possible score is 24 points, and the lowest 0. The closer the score comes to 24 points, the better your manager's feedback.

■ How does your manager's score compare to yours from the FAST Feedback Self-Evaluation?

PERSPECTIVE CHECK: Note that most people rate themselves higher than they rate their managers; thus it is a statistical probability that you rated yourself higher than your employees would. This is a fact worth keeping in mind.

CONCLUDED ●

≡ Appendix C ≡

The FAST Feedback Manager's Tool Kit

THE CONTENTS OF THE TOOL KIT

1. **GIVING FREQUENT FEEDBACK**
   Evaluating the Feedback Needs of Employees

2. **GIVING ACCURATE FEEDBACK**
   Checking Facts and Preparing Your Message

3. **GIVING SPECIFIC FEEDBACK**
   Clarifying Purpose and Assigning Action Steps

4. **GIVING TIMELY FEEDBACK**
   Anticipating Feedback and Making Time for It

THE FAST FEEDBACK MANAGER'S TOOL KIT contains the four exercises presented in *FAST Feedback*, Second Edition. These management and planning tools will help you put FAST coaching skills into action on a regular basis in your relationships with direct reports and valued co-workers. The tools are published as black-line masters, so feel free to make as many photocopies of them as you need. Please note that the tool kit is also available electronically on CD-interactive.

The FAST tools are highly versatile and include helpful worksheets. They can be used separately or in combination. Let's take a closer look.

1. GIVING FREQUENT FEEDBACK
Evaluating the Feedback Needs of Employees

This tool is presented in two parts; they can be used individually or together.

Part 1, Evaluating Different People—and Different Needs, will help you clarify the different feedback needs of your direct reports and other valued co-workers, so that you can begin to tune in to each person's unique frequency. It should be used periodically to assess and reassess the changing needs of the people you manage.

Part 2, Tuning In to Each Individual's Unique Frequency, will help you tune in more precisely to the unique frequency of a particular individual. This tool should be applied to every person you manage. Note that frequency is likely to change over time, so consider applying this tool whenever you feel you are getting "out of tune" with a particular direct report or other valued co-worker.

2. GIVING ACCURATE FEEDBACK
Checking Facts and Preparing Your Message

This tool will help you prepare a solid feedback message whenever you are evaluating a particular instance of performance of a direct report or valued co-worker. Use this tool to focus on the performance in question, to check your facts, to balance praise and criticism, and to refine your message.

3. GIVING SPECIFIC FEEDBACK
Clarifying Purpose and Assigning Action Steps

This tool will help you prepare a solid feedback message whenever you need to direct a particular individual on the next steps in any process. Use it to clarify your purpose; to set clear goals, deadlines, and parameters for the individual; and to refine your feedback message before delivering it.

4. GIVING TIMELY FEEDBACK
Anticipating Feedback and Making Time for It

This tool has two parts, which can be used separately or combined.

Part 1, Anticipating the Need for Feedback, will help you anticipate and plan for the feedback needs of those whom you manage. Use it once a week to identify who will be needing feedback on what matters and when.

Part 2, Your Weekly Schedule: Making Time for Feedback, is also a weekly planning tool, and is set up like a weekly planner. Use this, or your own weekly planner, to allocate specific blocks of time in your schedule to deliver the feedback needed by your direct reports and other valued co-workers.

Again, please keep in mind that FAST Feedback is about your day-to-day management relationships with direct reports and valued co-workers. Practicing FAST Feedback will transform these relationships and your role as manager. Those of us at RainmakerThinking wish you the best of the luck in the process.

> *Remember:*
> This tool kit is also available in electronic form on CD-interactive from HRD Press or RainmakerThinking.

1 Giving Frequent Feedback

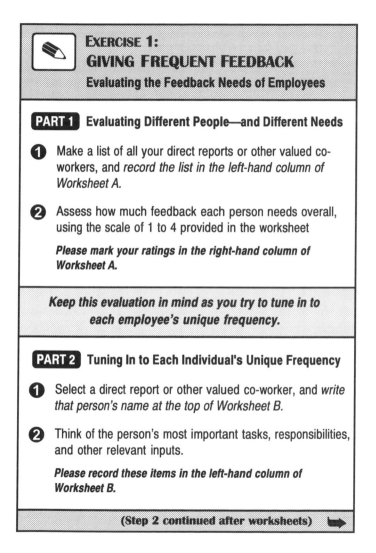

EXERCISE 1:
GIVING FREQUENT FEEDBACK
Evaluating the Feedback Needs of Employees

PART 1 Evaluating Different People—and Different Needs

1 Make a list of all your direct reports or other valued co-workers, and *record the list in the left-hand column of Worksheet A.*

2 Assess how much feedback each person needs overall, using the scale of 1 to 4 provided in the worksheet

Please mark your ratings in the right-hand column of Worksheet A.

Keep this evaluation in mind as you try to tune in to each employee's unique frequency.

PART 2 Tuning In to Each Individual's Unique Frequency

1 Select a direct report or other valued co-worker, and *write that person's name at the top of Worksheet B.*

2 Think of the person's most important tasks, responsibilities, and other relevant inputs.

Please record these items in the left-hand column of Worksheet B.

(Step 2 continued after worksheets) ➡

Exercise 1 — Worksheet A

Overall, how often do you think each direct report /co-worker needs feedback? Please circle your answer using this scale:

RATING SCALE

1. **Very Often**
2. **Somewhat Often**
3. **Somewhat Rarely**
4. **Very Rarely**

DIRECT REPORTS/VALUED CO-WORKERS	RATING
	1 2 3 4
	1 2 3 4
	1 2 3 4
	1 2 3 4
	1 2 3 4
	1 2 3 4
	1 2 3 4
	1 2 3 4
	1 2 3 4
	1 2 3 4
	1 2 3 4
	1 2 3 4

✎ Exercise 1 — Worksheet B

NAME: _____
(Direct Report/Valued Co-Worker)

How often do you think this person needs feedback on each task, responsibility, input? Please circle your answer using this scale:

RATING SCALE

1. More than once a day
2. Once a day
3. More than once a week
4. Once a week
5. Once every 2 weeks
6. Once a month

Tasks, Responsibilities, Inputs	RATING
1.	1 2 3 4 5 6
2.	1 2 3 4 5 6
3.	1 2 3 4 5 6

Go on to next page

Exercise 1 — Worksheet B (concluded)

RATING SCALE

1. More than once a day
2. Once a day
3. More than once a week

4. Once a week
5. Once every 2 weeks
6. Once a month

TASKS, RESPONSIBILITIES, INPUTS	RATING
4.	1 2 3 4 5 6
5.	1 2 3 4 5 6
6.	1 2 3 4 5 6
7.	1 2 3 4 5 6
8.	1 2 3 4 5 6

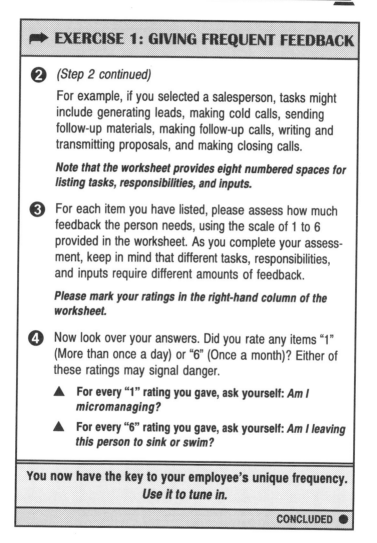

➡ **EXERCISE 1: GIVING FREQUENT FEEDBACK**

❷ *(Step 2 continued)*

For example, if you selected a salesperson, tasks might include generating leads, making cold calls, sending follow-up materials, making follow-up calls, writing and transmitting proposals, and making closing calls.

Note that the worksheet provides eight numbered spaces for listing tasks, responsibilities, and inputs.

❸ For each item you have listed, please assess how much feedback the person needs, using the scale of 1 to 6 provided in the worksheet. As you complete your assessment, keep in mind that different tasks, responsibilities, and inputs require different amounts of feedback.

Please mark your ratings in the right-hand column of the worksheet.

❹ Now look over your answers. Did you rate any items "1" (More than once a day) or "6" (Once a month)? Either of these ratings may signal danger.

▲ **For every "1" rating you gave, ask yourself:** *Am I micromanaging?*

▲ **For every "6" rating you gave, ask yourself:** *Am I leaving this person to sink or swim?*

You now have the key to your employee's unique frequency.
Use it to tune in.

CONCLUDED ●

2 Giving Accurate Feedback

EXERCISE 2:
GIVING ACCURATE FEEDBACK
Checking Facts and Preparing Your Message

Please follow the steps below.

1 Select a direct report or other valued co-worker, and *write that person's name on the accompanying worksheet.*

2 Take a moment to think about

— the person's overall work performance,
— his or her general strengths and weaknesses, and
— a few specific instances of work performance.

3 Select one work-performance matter that you can evaluate right now. Be specific. For example, you might focus on the performance of a specific task on a particular occasion.

Please record the matter in the appropriate space on the worksheet.

4 Take a moment to question your assumptions:

What do you really know about the matter you have selected for focus?

Now make a list of the facts that you consider to be most relevant to the matter.

Please record your list of key facts in the appropriate space on the worksheet.

(Steps continued after worksheet) ➡

Exercise 2 — Worksheet

FEEDBACK RECIPIENT: _____

(Direct Report/Valued Co-Worker)

THE PERFORMANCE MATTER UNDER FOCUS

1. RELEVANT FACTS ABOUT THE MATTER *Please list facts below.*	2. SOURCE OF EACH FACT *List sources; then note how sure you are about each fact.*

Go on to next page

Exercise 2 — Worksheet (concluded)

POSITIVES (PRAISE) *What elements merit praise?*	NEGATIVES (CRITICISM) *What elements require constructive criticism?*

REFINING THE MESSAGE

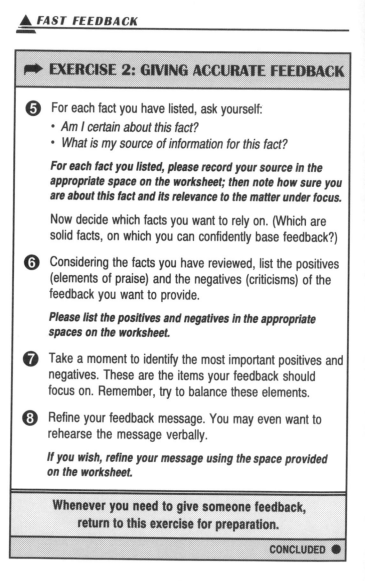

➡ EXERCISE 2: GIVING ACCURATE FEEDBACK

⑤ For each fact you have listed, ask yourself:
  - *Am I certain about this fact?*
  - *What is my source of information for this fact?*

For each fact you listed, please record your source in the appropriate space on the worksheet; then note how sure you are about this fact and its relevance to the matter under focus.

Now decide which facts you want to rely on. (Which are solid facts, on which you can confidently base feedback?)

⑥ Considering the facts you have reviewed, list the positives (elements of praise) and the negatives (criticisms) of the feedback you want to provide.

Please list the positives and negatives in the appropriate spaces on the worksheet.

⑦ Take a moment to identify the most important positives and negatives. These are the items your feedback should focus on. Remember, try to balance these elements.

⑧ Refine your feedback message. You may even want to rehearse the message verbally.

If you wish, refine your message using the space provided on the worksheet.

Whenever you need to give someone feedback, return to this exercise for preparation.

CONCLUDED ●

3 Giving Specific Feedback

Exercise 3:
GIVING SPECIFIC FEEDBACK
Clarifying Purpose and Assigning Action Steps

Please follow the steps below.

1 Select a direct report or other valued co-worker, and *write that person's name on the accompanying worksheet.*

2 Take a moment to think about
- — the person's overall work performance,
- — his or her general strengths and weaknesses, and
- — a few specific instances of the person's performance.

3 Select a particular matter that indicates the person needs coaching in "next steps"; that is, specific feedback about the matter.

For example, you might focus on the performance of a specific task. (If you also chose this person for the Accuracy exercise in Chapter 5, you can focus on the same issue you did there, or on a new one.)

Please record the issue in the appropriate space on the worksheet.

4 Clarify your purpose in terms as specific as you can make them. What tangible result do you hope to achieve by giving the feedback?

Please record your purpose in the appropriate space on the worksheet.

(Steps continued after worksheet) ➡

Exercise 3 — Worksheet

FEEDBACK RECIPIENT: _____
                                              (Direct Report/Valued Co-Worker)

THE PERFORMANCE MATTER UNDER FOCUS

CLARIFYING YOUR PURPOSE
What tangible results do you hope to achieve through the feedback?

PREPARING YOUR FEEDBACK (COACHING "NEXT STEPS")

TANGIBLE GOALS	GOAL DEADLINES	PARAMETERS, GUIDELINES

Go on to next page

Exercise 3 — Worksheet (concluded)

PREPARING YOUR FEEDBACK (Continue list as needed.)

TANGIBLE GOALS	GOAL DEADLINES	PARAMETERS, GUIDELINES

REFINING THE MESSAGE

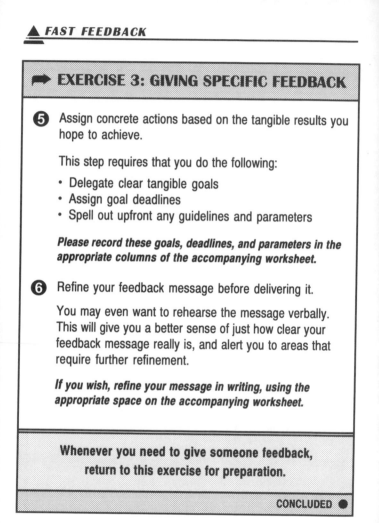

➡ **EXERCISE 3: GIVING SPECIFIC FEEDBACK**

⑤ Assign concrete actions based on the tangible results you hope to achieve.

This step requires that you do the following:

- Delegate clear tangible goals
- Assign goal deadlines
- Spell out upfront any guidelines and parameters

Please record these goals, deadlines, and parameters in the appropriate columns of the accompanying worksheet.

⑥ Refine your feedback message before delivering it.

You may even want to rehearse the message verbally. This will give you a better sense of just how clear your feedback message really is, and alert you to areas that require further refinement.

If you wish, refine your message in writing, using the appropriate space on the accompanying worksheet.

Whenever you need to give someone feedback, return to this exercise for preparation.

CONCLUDED ●

4 Giving Timely Feedback

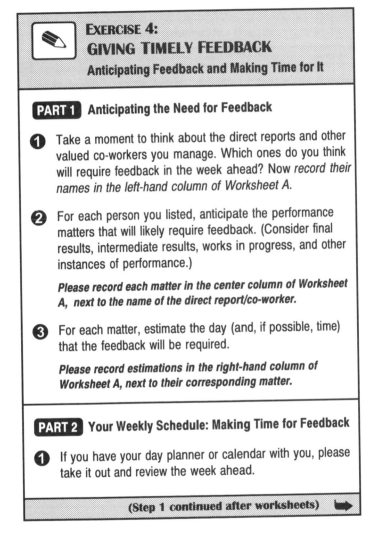

EXERCISE 4:
GIVING TIMELY FEEDBACK
Anticipating Feedback and Making Time for It

PART 1 Anticipating the Need for Feedback

1 Take a moment to think about the direct reports and other valued co-workers you manage. Which ones do you think will require feedback in the week ahead? Now *record their names in the left-hand column of Worksheet A.*

2 For each person you listed, anticipate the performance matters that will likely require feedback. (Consider final results, intermediate results, works in progress, and other instances of performance.)

Please record each matter in the center column of Worksheet A, next to the name of the direct report/co-worker.

3 For each matter, estimate the day (and, if possible, time) that the feedback will be required.

Please record estimations in the right-hand column of Worksheet A, next to their corresponding matter.

PART 2 Your Weekly Schedule: Making Time for Feedback

1 If you have your day planner or calendar with you, please take it out and review the week ahead.

(Step 1 continued after worksheets) ➡

Exercise 4 — Worksheet A

WHO WILL NEED FEEDBACK? (Please list.)	WHAT MATTERS WILL REQUIRE FEEDBACK? (Please list.)	WHEN? (Please list day and time.)
	))) ➡	))) ➡
	))) ➡	))) ➡
	))) ➡	))) ➡
	))) ➡	))) ➡
	))) ➡	))) ➡
	))) ➡	))) ➡
	))) ➡	))) ➡
	))) ➡	))) ➡

Exercise 4 — Worksheet B

Use the daily calendar below to schedule time for feedback in the week ahead.

THE WEEK AHEAD

SUNDAY

MONDAY

TUESDAY

WEDNESDAY

THURSDAY

FRIDAY

SATURDAY

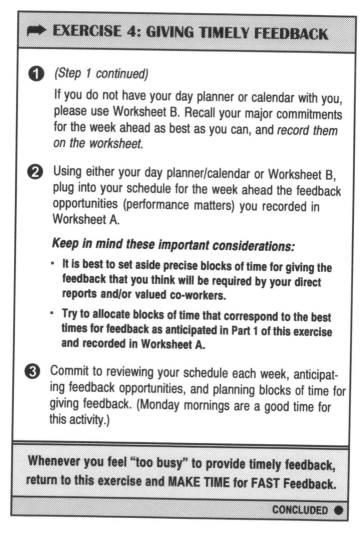

➡ EXERCISE 4: GIVING TIMELY FEEDBACK

❶ *(Step 1 continued)*

If you do not have your day planner or calendar with you, please use Worksheet B. Recall your major commitments for the week ahead as best as you can, and *record them on the worksheet.*

❷ Using either your day planner/calendar or Worksheet B, plug into your schedule for the week ahead the feedback opportunities (performance matters) you recorded in Worksheet A.

Keep in mind these important considerations:

- It is best to set aside precise blocks of time for giving the feedback that you think will be required by your direct reports and/or valued co-workers.
- Try to allocate blocks of time that correspond to the best times for feedback as anticipated in Part 1 of this exercise and recorded in Worksheet A.

❸ Commit to reviewing your schedule each week, anticipating feedback opportunities, and planning blocks of time for giving feedback. (Monday mornings are a good time for this activity.)

Whenever you feel "too busy" to provide timely feedback, return to this exercise and MAKE TIME for FAST Feedback.

CONCLUDED ●

Standardized
FAST Feedback Memos
SAMPLE TEMPLATES

THE FOLLOWING tips and sample templates will help you use the FAST Feedback method for optimum results.

1. Put FAST Feedback into writing.

Putting feedback into writing holds managers to a higher standard of quality. It also:

▲ Diminishes the chances that employees will misunderstand the feedback

▲ Allows for greater standardization

▲ Enables record keeping

2. Standardize the format.

To reduce feedback-transaction time, establish a standard format for employees to request feedback and for managers to respond. Select one or more forms from the samples provided in this appendix, or use the samples as models for creating your own forms.

3. Whatever you do, keep it simple.

A feedback form needs space for:

▲ Employee's name

▲ Manager's name

▲ Time and date of feedback request

▲ Time and date of feedback provided

▲ Employee's feedback request—description of query, work in progress, final result, or performance in question

▲ Manager's accurate and specific feedback, including action steps

4. Use a portfolio system.

Keep records of FAST Feedback memos by using a portfolio system. Employees may be given responsibility for maintaining their portfolios as long as they remain with the organization (or wish to keep open the option of returning).

Managers should retain copies of memos they consider particularly significant, and such copies should be saved in employee files. These copies may be an important resource for longer-term employee evaluation as well.

5. Do it electronically.

The same approach may be used to deliver FAST Feedback memos electronically, and standard templates may be prepared in electronic form for an internal messaging system or standard e-mail.

Communicating electronically may have some pitfalls (the lack of face-to-face communication, with cues such as body language, vocal tone, facial expression), but it has tremendous advantages too. For example, you can store a large portfolio of contemporaneous performance evaluations in a manner that allows easy compilation and integration into longer-term reviews.

SAMPLE FAST FEEDBACK FORM 1

TO (Manager):	BY ☐ FAX ☐ E-MAIL ☐ INTERNAL MAIL
FROM (Employee):	TIME: DATE:

Employee: Please describe **(CIRCLE ONE OF THE FOLLOWING)** :

QUERY / WORK IN PROGRESS / FINAL RESULT / PERFORMANCE

☐ See attached.

Manager: Please provide **(CIRCLE ONE OF THE FOLLOWING)** :

ANSWER / INFORMATION / REVISION / SIGN-OFF / OTHER ACTION STEP

☐ See attached.

Returned by:	TIME: DATE:

Signature _____

SAMPLE FAST FEEDBACK FORM 2

TO:	BY ☐ FAX ☐ E-MAIL ☐ INTERNAL MAIL
FROM:	TIME: DATE:

SALES ASSOCIATE

TASKS	RESULTS	FEEDBACK
Adding names to prospect list		
Cold calls		
Follow-up calls		
Sending follow-up materials		
Proposals and bids		
Scheduling in-person meetings		
In-person meetings		
Closing deals		
Follow-up calls to check on customer satisfaction		

Returned by:	TIME: DATE:
Signature _____	

SAMPLE FAST FEEDBACK FORM 3

TO:	BY ☐ FAX ☐ E-MAIL ☐ INTERNAL MAIL
FROM:	TIME: DATE:

(Customize to the tasks and responsibilities of any job)

	RESULTS	FEEDBACK

Returned by:	TIME: DATE:
Signature _____	

SAMPLE FAST FEEDBACK FORM 4

TO:	BY ☐ FAX ☐ E-MAIL ☐ INTERNAL MAIL
FROM:	TIME: DATE:

(Customize to the tasks and responsibilities of any job)

RESULT TO BE EVALUATED	POSITIVE FEEDBACK	PLEASE MAKE FOLLOWING IMPROVEMENTS

Returned by:	TIME: DATE:
Signature _____	

SAMPLE FAST FEEDBACK FORM 5

TO (Manager):	BY ☐ FAX ☐ E-MAIL ☐ INTERNAL MAIL
FROM (Employee):	**TIME:** **DATE:**

Results to be evaluated:

☐ See attached.

Please make the following revisions by indicated deadline:

Please keep the following in mind for similar projects:

Please consider the following training opportunity:

Returned by:	**TIME:**
Signature _____	**DATE:**